RAISING PRESIDENTS

The Unique Perspective of a Stay-at-home Dad and Working Mom on Parenting in Today's World

by Russell Clark

©2020
Endorsed by The National At-Home Dad Network
Copyright & publishing rights owned by the author
Author contact: russellclarkauthor@yahoo.com
Cover Design by John Lee

"Russell Clark's Raising Presidents *is an engaging, lighthearted take on the life of a stay at-home dad and his family. With his unique background and what has made him the father he is today, Russell's family exemplifies the joys, frustrations, and obstacles that often face a family with a father as the primary caregiver.*

Russell makes it clear that there are many dads like him, who share in these common struggles, yet are changing the face of fatherhood, one family at a time. Stay at-home dads are part of a brotherhood of fatherhood, often misunderstood in today's turbulent times. But hopefully Russell's story will resonate with those who are experiencing this role for the first time, and invigorate many more men to reconsider their role as a father.

I could easily relate to the feelings expressed about the infant and toddler years, the off-hand comments of family members or strangers, and the struggles with emotions that come from taking on a non-traditional role in today's society. Russell is able to bring rays of sunshine to those who may feel in darkness, assuring the skeptical and cynical that parenting as a dad can have a positive impact, not only on themselves, but more especially on the ones they love the most - their kids and spouse."

~ Jonathan Heisey-Grove
Stay at-home dad of two boys, 13 and 7
President of The National At-Home Dad Network

"Finally a book that speaks directly to me about the role as a stay-at-home dad! Russell pulls no punches in addressing the hurdles he and his wife have faced in their family dynamic. Each chapter captures the inside look of the new modern father and the truth of how dads in the primary care role are able to parent at the same level as a mom. There are good conversation starters to put both parents on the same page. Also, an introduction to an organization — The National At Home Dad Network — that gives stay-at-home dads a place to be shown Advocacy, Community, Education and Support. I am pleased to say that this book is a must-read for any father thinking about being a stay-at-home dad."

*~ Brock Lusch (fellow at-home dad)
Podcast Host of The NOMADad Podcast
Founder of the Cincinnati Dads Group
Board Member of The National At Home Dad Network*

"Raising Presidents is a raw sharing of the author's experiences as a stay-at-home dad as he and his wife begin their journey of parenthood. Through the various difficulties of parenting in a world that views dads as just tokens in the process, Clark shares his frustrations and joys of being a dad who just so happens to have the full-time job of raising his daughters. This book is a simple and engaging read for anyone interested in understanding the realities stay-at-home dads face and how important the father role is in raising competent and successful kids."

~ Dr. Gladys Childs, Ph.D., Dean of Freshman Success at Texas Wesleyan University

"The book "Raising Presidents" is an enjoyable and honest look at the joys and challenges of parenting from a stay-at-home dads' perspective. Russell shares his real-life journey and tells it like it is all the way through. I found myself laughing and feeling sad as he shares the moments and lessons from his experience raising two daughters as a stay-at-home-dad. I found the book to be easy to read, easy to relate to, funny and heartfelt. I enjoyed reading about Russell's faith and family, and how things have developed for them over the years.

Thanks for sharing the not-so-easy challenges and real life situations that any parent can identify with. The SAHD advice is helpful and spot-on. Also sharing the expectations we have for ourselves and others and also the working-mom's perspective was helpful too. I enjoyed the points about parenting and fatherhood, and the dads' point of view about society's expectations and roles for both parents and how that is changing (for the better) in today's society.

I enjoyed the team work parenting approach that Russell shared, and the kindness and values and lessons he's sharing with his daughters and those around him.
Thanks for writing this book! I'm sure others will find it a reassuring perspective on how challenging and wonderful parenting is at the same time."

~ John Francis, Founding Father of Father's Eve

RAISING PRESIDENTS
The Unique Perspective of a Stay-at-home Dad and Working Mom on Parenting in Today's World
by Russell Clark

Table of Contents

Chapter 1 – Dinosaurs and Stairs and Miscarriages and Slot Machines

Chapter 2 – Baptism

Chapter 3 – The Chaos of Raising Airports

Chapter 4 – The Stay-at-Home Dad: Parenting is Not Just For Moms

Chapter 5 – The Working Mom: A Mother's Sacrifice

Chapter 6 – Longing for the Moments

Chapter 7 – Feminist Father: My Future is Female

Chapter 8 – My Parenting Complaints are Outweighing My Joy

Chapter 9 – My New Best Friend

Chapter 10 – Beloved

Chapter 11 – Friendship Day

Chapter 12 – Chrysalis

*For my parents,
Gil and Mary Clark,
who were the first to show me
what unconditional love looks
like.*

Chapter 1
Dinosaurs and Stairs and Miscarriages and Slot Machines

Hyper mode: activated.

My curly-haired, independent daughter is doing circles around the living area with her scooter at ludicrous speed – giggling all the way – while our dog, Crowder, barks in frustration at the ruckus she is causing that doesn't include him.

This is the daily routine right before bedtime to activate hyper mode. It's the last-ditch effort to prove she's not tired by doing laps with her scooter or having a dance party or treating me like her own personal trampoline.

"Kennedy, two more minutes until bedtime," my beautiful, strong, perfect,

wants-just-five-minutes-to-herself-before-bed wife, Shannon, proclaims.

"Ten more minutes, mommy."

"Two."

"Ten, mommy. *Pleeeeeeaaasssseee.*"

"You can have ten if you go potty right now."

"But I don't need to go potty!"

"Then, it's time for bed."

The kid jumps off her scooter in protest and falls to the floor, going limp.

"Go! Now!" I chimed in.

She slowly stands up and heads in the direction of the bathroom. She is distracted after two steps. She stops to properly examine the toy she found on the ground like a scientist finding a ground-breaking discovery.

"Bathroom! Now!", my wife states, as she pauses to finish her glass of wine, "What does Daniel Tiger [1] say?"

"If you have to go potty, stop and go right away! Flush and wash and be on your way!**" we all sing, like an embarrassing, annoying family that sings kids' songs together.

Kennedy sighs as she walks like a sloth to the restroom and loudly opens the toilet seat.

"I got this feeling inside my bones! It goes 'lectric, baby, when I turn it on!" [2]

All potty breaks require renditions of the complete *Trolls* soundtrack.

"I did it! I went potty!"

"Good job!" Shannon and I say in unison.

"Now, wipe really good. Flush and wash and be on your way," I remind her what Daniel Tiger says. "And hang the towel up!"

My daughter stops in her tracks and goes back to hang the towel up. *Why do kids never hang the freaking towel up?*

"Tell mommy night-night."

She has to come my direction and plow herself down on my stomach on her way to give mommy a hug.

"I love you this much..." my wife joyfully tells our daughter as she holds her hands tight together.

"I love you this much..." she adds getting louder and opening her hands wider.

"I love you *THIS* much!" she smiles as her arms are open wide and she gives Kennedy a big hug.

Kennedy giggles as she is embraced in her mother's arms. I smile knowing this moment never gets old. Even though it's *twenty minutes later* from the time we were arguing with her about having *two* more minutes before bedtime.

Shannon secretly whispers in Kennedy's ears: "*Ask Daddy if he'll be a dinosaur.*"

For a kid who never wants to go to bed the dinosaur is the secret weapon.

"Daddy, will you please be a dinosaur?"

Even when I'm engrossed by the baseball game or something mind-numbing on my phone, the dinosaur is the cue.

I pretend I don't hear her.

"Daddy, will you PLEASE be a dinosaur?"

I shorten my arms slowly and stand up, ready to attack.

"You better hurry before Daddy Dinosaur gets you!" my wife gleefully insists.

The 42-pound four-year old sprints up the stairs, giggling all the way as I run behind her with my dinosaur roars.

"Rooooar! You better hurry! Roar!! I'm going to get you!" my deep dinosaur voice screamed.

//

We used to be so nervous about her going up and down the stairs. As soon as she discovered the stairs when she was barely crawling, she could be halfway up before we realized where she was. The baby gate only created a bigger challenge for her to escape and find her way up.

Crawling. Walking. Sprinting.

A lot has happened in now seven years of going up and down stairs being Daddy Dinosaur.

Before Kennedy came into this world, I remember running up a different set of stairs to find her mama.

//

"Whatever you do – don't forget where you left me." Shannon begged her directionally-challenged boyfriend, as I was running back to our room on the cruise ship for a minute to secretly grab her engagement ring.

"I won't."

I did.

After I nervously changed into nice slacks, a button-down shirt, and tie and stuffed the engagement ring in my pocket, I became more and more nervous running up and down stairwell after stairwell trying to find where I left my girlfriend. *It was a big cruise ship, dammit!*

"This is the most important time in my life and I can't even find her!" I said to myself as I began sweating profusely, frantically searching the ship.

The sun had gone down completely by the time I found my way back to her.

I shocked her standing behind her in the dark.

"What are you doing?! Why are you dressed like that?! *What took you so long*?!!"

As I tried to calm my girlfriend down (and myself), I honestly don't even remember what I said in the next few minutes. It was probably something mushy that I'm sure I planned out in my head over and over.

Shannon wanted me to give her a good story to tell about our engagement. I knew I wanted to propose to her on the cruise. Her parents took us on this cruise for our Christmas present in 2004 with her sister, Kacie, and her boyfriend, Chad.

A year earlier was when I met Shannon through Chad and Kacie. Chad was my best friend in college. Kacie wanted Shannon to meet Chad's "crazy friend, Russell" to "show her a good time." Shannon had been dating someone in college who she found out was engaged to someone else, and both of her paternal grandparents had passed away earlier that year. She was coming home for Christmas break so we all arranged to go bowling one evening.

I actually got lost the first time I was going to her house. I guess I tend to get lost at important moments in my life before I find my way. I went the wrong way on the highway for about 10 minutes before I realized I was going the wrong direction.

Chad and I were wearing Fred and Barney Flintstone[3] Bowling shirts and fake mustaches the day I met Shannon. Chad and I taught the girls "speed bowling" where it's not about your bowling score, but how quickly you can get up from your seat, bowl, and make it back to your seat. We laughed until our cheeks hurt that day.

We even went back to their house and watched Chad and my *two-hour* road trip video to South Dakota. This is the most mind-numbing video ever – like an old *Jackass*[4] show on steroids. It was full of insane antics, crazy hats and outfits at Mount Rushmore, and a dead bird's burial.

As I reflected on our first evening together, I couldn't stop smiling. She wasn't looking for a boyfriend, and I wasn't looking for a girlfriend because I had just ended a relationship with an on again/off again girlfriend. But I guess because we weren't interested in dating that we let loose and just had a great time.

I thought, "If this girl likes me after seeing me at my absolute craziest, she *must* be the one!"

Two days later Chad and I were at a college event when the girls called us to go to the zoo. I practically did flips I was so excited. In fact, I think I did do a flip and injured myself.

Shannon and I spent every day together the rest of Christmas break. When we weren't together in person, we were on the phone for two or more hours. After two weeks, we professed our love for each other. It was definitely love at first sight.

Shannon and I are complete opposites. She's the "crazy business lady" who follows all the rules and is realistic about limitations in day-to-day life. I'm the laid back dreamer who always thinks we can do more than we can. We are the perfect balance. I've taught her to be more spontaneous and she's taught me to think critically.

I fell in love with her because she was so independent and strong. In my previous relationship, my girlfriend needed me to be her minister and support system. Shannon had such a strong head on her shoulder she didn't need me for anything.

She *chose* me.

Back on the cruise ship a year later, I was down on one knee professing how I want to spend the rest of my life with my crazy business lady.

She said, "Yes! Yes! Yes!" and we embraced and spun around. We didn't know that people were watching on the deck above us and started clapping for us. We found Shannon's parents and Chad and Kacie and told them the good news. Chad had a few drinks on the cruise ship already so he was telling everyone on the ship: *"Did you hear the good news?! These two just got engaged!!"*

He sometimes told the same people the good news two or three…or four times.

This was the first day of a seven-day cruise so we were pretty well known for the rest of the cruise.

And I think I gave Shannon a good engagement story to tell.

//

When we married, we wanted to spend some time on our own, earning our bachelor's and master's degrees and traveling some before we had kids. It was six years later we decided to try to have a baby. This resulted in Shannon having three miscarriages.

Miscarriages.

It's like a taboo thing to talk about. I never knew how many people have had miscarriages before we went through it ourselves.

It's probably because people say the most *God-awful* things when you tell them.

"It wasn't the right time to have a baby."
"God needed an angel."
"This happened because something was wrong with the baby and God is preparing something better."

"Everything happens for a reason."

Someone even said, "*You'll get over this.*"

F--- you.

Don't tell people that experienced such a loss any of those things. Just don't tell them anything. Just cry with them. Just hug them. Just be there.

There's no reasoning or logic or pithy statements of faith that will explain the pain of losing a child, no matter how early in the pregnancy it was.

With Shannon's third miscarriage, she had to have an operation. I was a pastor at the time and I was thinking, "I sit with people during times like these. Who will sit with me if I'm the pastor?"

My lay leader from my church, Jim, met me at the hospital. And my mother-in-law, Trish, flew from Texas to Florida to be with us at the hospital. Our friends, Tom and Michelle, both worked in the medical field and they were our listening ear when we were completely broken. They spent the most time crying with us during each of the miscarriages. For this, we will forever be grateful.

Let me tell you this pain is not something any parent ever gets over. It stays with you.

A mother never forgets what it felt like to have that baby inside of her. A father never forgets the joy of becoming a new daddy. To have that stripped away just once is unbearable.

Three times was unthinkable.

Being a dad had always been a dream of mine – a destiny I felt like I was called to at a young age. Like girls dream of the perfect wedding day, I dreamt of one day being a dad. My mom was a preschool teacher and I was always helping her care for kids at our home growing up. In college, I was a youth minister and I adored working with youth and children helping them to believe in God and to believe in themselves.

Shannon and I did all the genetic testing to find out what was wrong with us. *Nothing* was wrong with us. Every test said we were perfectly healthy. All we found out was I have an extra chromosome, which really meant nothing in the grand scheme of things. I called it my superhero chromosome because apparently I'm a mutant.

We were considering adoption or doing IVF (In Vitro Fertilization). But I told Shannon we need a break because we are too stressed and grieving to know the right thing to do.

//

This led us to another cruise ship. We went on a cruise with Shannon's dad, Kip, his new wife-to-be, Lynn, and her daughter and niece.

Shannon had a couples massage scheduled for us the first day of the cruise. The massage was double-booked and Shannon couldn't get the massage she desperately needed. Everything hit her like a ton of bricks and she broke down crying.

"Why can't anything go right for us?!" I thought.

Kip took Shannon gambling for a while. I took a minute to cool down and get a drink. Later I met them at the casino and sat down on my own at a slot machine.

I remember thinking, "This slot machine can't bring me joy. I just want things to go right for myself and my wife. *We just want a baby.*"

After three quarters, the slot machine hit the jackpot! I won $1600 the first day of the cruise!

Lynn's daughter, Jen, and niece, Lisa, were on the cruise with us too and I was buying everyone's drinks the rest of the day!

We went to a comedy club that evening and got Kip plastered. He was hilarious as we were eating late-night drunk pizza. That was the best part of the cruise.

At the end of the cruise, I sarcastically told Kip, *"It's just wrong leaving the cruise with more money than I came here with."*

"Oh, shut up," he replied with a jealous grin.

//

It was a year later from this cruise – after going through our third miscarriage and giving up hope that we would ever have a baby – that Shannon became pregnant for the fourth time.

With three previous miscarriages, Shannon was doing everything the doctor told her – taking prenatal vitamins and staying as stress-free as possible and avoiding anything that was unhealthy for the baby.

We climbed a lot of stairs to become parents. When all seemed lost and we felt like we were going the wrong direction, we found our way.

Our story is one where joy and pain, laughter and grief, hope and loss all happen simultaneously.

//

As I ran up the stairs roaring like a dinosaur, I always caught Kennedy at the top of the stairs. I picked her up and tickled her and kissed her neck.

"Daddy dinosaur got you! Now let's brush your teeth…"

Typically we would sing songs and make silly faces in the mirror as she brushed her teeth. Shannon would yell from downstairs, *"You two are having too much fun when you're supposed to be getting ready for bed!"*

"Daddy, be a dinosaur again!," Kennedy would proclaim as she ran to her bedroom and we both ignored mommy's plea from downstairs.

"Roooooaaaarrrr!"

One of our favorite things has been for her to stand up in her bed and I act like I'm "using the force" from *Star Wars*[5] and she fearlessly falls backwards on to her bed.

"Do that again, Daddy! Do that again!"

After a few (fifty) times of using the force, I would lay down with her in bed to read her a book. Some nights I would just make up a story so she'd go to bed faster. Or that's what I told myself.

"Daddy, tell a bedtime story..."

"Once upon a time there were 5 friends — Beast, Lambie, Genie, Mike Wazowski[6], & Kennedy — after a fun day, they all laid down in bed, got tucked in, & went night night. The. end."

"Now I want to tell a story!"

"Ok..."

"Once upon a time there were *twenty* friends..."

"Oh man...this just backfired..."

Then, it took her forever to pick out the stuffed animal she wanted to sleep with. She would change her mind and pick a different one. Then go back to the original one. Then want more than one. Then want every stuffed animal she owned in bed with her.

"Let's say your prayer now."

Shannon and I have said the same prayer with her at bedtime since she was born.

"Lord, thank you for our baby. Help her to keep growing and learning and talking. Help her to know she can be whoever she wants to be. And we will love her no matter who she becomes. Amen…

"I love you sweet pea. Now go to sleep. *Puh-lease*."

"I love you Daddy."

I hit the jackpot.

Chapter 2
Baptism

When Shannon was in labor with Kennedy, she would muster up all her strength to push when it was time. Shannon asked me to put my hand on her chest to help calm her down in between contractions. She often asks me to put my hand on her chest during times of stress.

"Just...breathe..." I calmly said as I focused on breathing calmly myself.

After Kennedy was born, the nurse had my newborn on the table taking measurements and poking and prodding her. Kennedy was highly uncomfortable and crying at the top of her lungs. I put my hand on her chest – as I had just done with her mother – and my sister-in-law, Kacie, said, *"O my God! She calmed down simply by your touch!"*

This is one of the greatest memories during the birth of my firstborn child.

A moment I will treasure forever.

//

In my first book, *Loser*[7], I told the story of Ms. Eva.

Every time I saw her I would ask her:

"How are you Ms. Eva?"

"I'm *mean*!", she would respond.

This is a testament to her strength and tenacity and humor.

On my last Sunday serving as pastor at First United Methodist Church in Reddick, Florida, Ms. Eva couldn't make it to church that Sunday. At this time, Ms. Eva was the oldest living member of this church. After Shannon and I all said our goodbyes to everyone at the church, we went to see Ms. Eva at her home.

This was the last time we would see her.

We told her we would always treasure the guardian angels she would make for us at Christmas.

I told her to always stay *"mean."*

Shannon was 7 months pregnant with Kennedy at the time we were visiting with Ms. Eva.

All 3 of Shannon's miscarriages happened while I was the pastor in Reddick. I'm not sure if Ms. Eva knew the trouble we had experienced trying to have a child or not.

But during that visit I remember one of the last things Ms. Eva said to us as we hugged her goodbye was that she was praying for our baby *every day*.

//

A couple months later after that meeting with Ms. Eva, Kennedy was born at 1:41pm.

Ms. Eva passed away at 12:00 noon.

Considering the time difference, this would mean Ms. Eva passed away about a few hours before Kennedy was born.

Kayla, her granddaughter, contacted me late that afternoon to let me know that Ms. Eva had passed away. As Shannon and I were talking about everything that evening, adoring our new baby girl, we noticed the nurse watching over us overnight was named, Eva.

Of all the names, it was Eva again watching over our baby girl.

Just like the guardian angels Ms. Eva would give out at Christmas time, it seemed as though Ms. Eva was our own guardian angel.

It seems that through all the miscarriages and asking God, "Why?" and wondering why we're being hit with all these curveballs, *God knew exactly what He was doing.*

Ms. Eva was praying for our baby girl every day. *We had our own guardian angel.*

Just as my hand had calmed my newborn's heart, God calmed our hearts in that moment when we recognized we were touched by His grace.

The nurse, Ms. Eva, told Shannon and me that she could tell we are doing a great job with our newborn because we are so calm and collected. She said newborns will respond to the attitude of their parents.

//

I wish we could say we are always so calm and collected. I wish I still had that special touch to calm down my child when she became possessed by the demon, *Toddlerhood*.

Being a parent and staying calm are not synonymous.

There have been those moments when I'm standing up peeing in the toilet and I'm fighting off the kid with my leg who is trying to walk into my pee stream.

There have been times when I've been sick with a cold and I've locked the kid and myself in her playroom and let her trash the playroom with all her toys so I could just lay on the floor and try to recuperate.

There have been times when I'm doing my business in our tiny bathroom and the kid brings her *Paw Patrol*[8] cars, our two dogs, and her *Doc McStuffins*[9] kit. She then proceeds to give the dogs and me a "check-up" while I'm doing my business.

"It stinks in here, Daddy!"

"Well, do you think I could get some privacy, kiddo?"

"No, daddy! You need a check-up!"

"Why is everything you own in here…and the dogs?!"

"Just…breathe, Daddy, while I feel your heartbeat!"

//

There are also stressful times when your baby is sick and you don't know what is wrong. There's honestly nothing worse as a parent.

The scariest moment for us as parents was when Kennedy was just two weeks old.

We were sitting at home ready for a peaceful evening watching college football when Kennedy's temperature started spiking. As it continued to climb, we decided we needed to go to the children's hospital.

Cook's Children's Hospital in Fort Worth, Texas, is one of the best hospitals we've ever encountered.

They were quick in analyzing our baby. They took her vitals and asked us a million questions trying to figure out what was wrong.

One of the most heartbreaking moments was when they gave her a spinal tap. They said we didn't need to be in the room for it, but we didn't want to leave our baby. Now we know why they said that. Kennedy gave out the loudest, most terrifying screams I've ever heard. It completely shook all of us. It's something we'll never forget.

Turns out Kennedy had a E.coli bacterial infection. To this date, we don't know how it happened. It could have happened during delivery or because someone didn't wash their hands very well. It could have come from anywhere.

She was in the hospital for ten terrifying days.

If it weren't for everyone praying for our baby girl and visiting us and making us take a break to eat something, we might have lost it completely.

There's nothing worse than your baby being in the hospital.

Thankfully, she recovered, and has never had any major issue like that again.

But the stress of that time still makes our hearts beat faster when we recall it.

//

Another stressful time was when my teething, seven-month old baby was awake at 3:00 in the morning.

I had been up for two hours.
Two. Hours. In the middle of the night.

I did everything in my power to get her to go back to sleep.

I gave her Tylenol.
I fed her a bottle.
I rocked her.
I sang to her.
I turned on *Mickey Mouse Clubhouse*[10] upstairs.

I was frantic trying to get my baby to go back to sleep without waking up my wife or my mother-in-law, who was staying with us that night.

And. She. Just. Kept. *Crying!*

I was becoming increasingly frustrated.

Then she had a dirty diaper. I tiptoed downstairs to get a clean diaper.

I tiptoed back upstairs only to find that she *peed all over herself.* I stomped downstairs to get a clean outfit. *(I was still new at this daddy thing.)*

I made my way back upstairs only to find her screaming at the top of her lungs again and I said out loud to myself:

"This is it. This is the worst night of my entire life."

Two hours in the middle of the night and I was at my wit's end.

And at that very moment, my mother-in-law, Trish, almost on cue, showed up and said very calmly, *"Give me the baby."*

As she started to rock her, I tried to get out words to tell her, "No, this is my responsibility, Trish. You go back to bed. I can take care of her."

But the words wouldn't come out.

My body was so exhausted and my brain was all-but-gone. And this other part of me was saying, "*I can't. I can't do this anymore.*"

Within a few minutes my mother-in-law had calmed Kennedy down, and she fell asleep.

This was the first time my mother-in-law had stayed with us since Kennedy was born. She just so happened to be staying with us that evening after we *convinced* her to stay the night at dinner time earlier that evening.

And I really don't know how I would have made it through the night without her help.

She was a *Godsend*.

That night – again – we were touched by grace.

//

I had the privilege of conducting Kennedy's baptism myself at my father-in-law's house. His wife, Lynn, inherited the house from her parents.

It's one of my favorite places.

We call it "The Hill" because the house is on a hill that overlooks a beautiful landscape of trees and grass that emotes a peaceful serenity. Occasionally, we can see deer eating from the feeding trough in the distance.

We had all of our family and friends present for Kennedy's baptism on The Hill on a beautiful Sunday morning.

Baptism is a sign of renewal. It's this sign of a new birth or new life. Baptism is an outward, public display of this inner presence of God's grace in our lives.

It's a gift freely given, which is why it's called grace.

Just as this water in baptism cleanses us, God cleanses us of our sins and renews us to be a different person, to tell a different story, to see a different perspective, to receive this gift before we even knew what was happening.

It's a gift freely given before we even knew of God's love. It's prevenient grace, which means it's grace that is for us *before* we knew of who God is.

Just as we drink water as nourishment and fulfillment, the Holy Spirit enters our bodies and souls to fill us up with a new life, a new way of looking at ourselves, a new person that has a life worth living, a story worth telling, a miracle in our midst, a life touched by grace.

And God has this grace already available to us because Jesus paid the price for us on the cross many, many years ago. This grace is freely offered here and now.

This is why it was important for Shannon and me as Kennedy's parents to baptize her as an infant because this is about what God has already done for us, what God promises to do for us, and what God is doing for us this day. This grace has always been with her, even before she was born.

God's grace is available for Kennedy as it is for us before we can even comprehend what God is doing. God is already creating a beautiful story for Kennedy to tell.

Just as water helps flowers to grow and blossom, this grace and love of Christ will help Kennedy to grow into the woman of God she has been created to be.

And it is my and Shannon's responsibility as Kennedy's parents to remind her of the life God has in store for her when she deals with bullies telling her she is someone different. At those moments she feels all hope is lost, it is our time to put our hands on her and remind her of how she has been touched by grace her entire life.

She can be reminded of how her parents longed for a child and after three miscarriages she was the answer to our prayers – our rainbow baby.

She can hear about the time her father calmed her mother and herself during the time of her birth simply by his touch.

She can know she's always had a guardian angel in Ms. Eva.

She can hear the funny stories of the times she stressed us out as parents – and how she has taught us so much about laughing through the stress in our lives.

She can know that throughout her life family and friends have poured their hearts out in prayer for her, like when she was sick at two weeks old with an E.coli infection.

She can hear the story of when her Mimi saved her father from a stressful evening when she was teething at seven months old – and he learned a little bit more about grace.

She can be reminded of when all of her family was present for her baptism, recognizing how God's grace has been present throughout her life before she even recognized it.

And she will know then she has been and will always be touched by this grace.

"Kennedy Clark, I baptize you in the name of the Father, and of the Son, and of the Holy Spirit. The Holy Spirit work within you, that being born through water and the Spirit, you may be a faithful disciple of Jesus Christ. Amen."

Chapter 3
The Chaos of Raising Airports

Shannon: Your little sister is in my belly. You can talk to her and she can hear you. Is there something you want to say to her?

Kennedy: Do you want to go to Chick-fil-a with me?

When we found out Shannon was pregnant with our 2nd child, I soon sought the advice of my dad friends in Kentucky. My buddy, Scott, was quick to chime in:

"Going from one to two kids isn't a little harder…it's so much worse!"

Truer words have never been spoken. From the moment Shannon told me she was pregnant, we've been unraveling a tangled ball of chaos ever since.

Shannon and I had discussed having a 2nd child, but we were ready to call it quits when an important opportunity came up with her career. Of course the week of her interview we found out she was pregnant. I'm not saying that Shannon slapped me for getting her pregnant, but when she told me she was pregnant it wasn't all cupcakes and rainbows. I was excited, but I had to contain my emotions because Shannon was nervous of how she would balance a potential new and very busy role at work along with being pregnant.

I told some of my friends that they should teach kids not to get their girlfriends pregnant because you are *not* ready for pregnancy hormones until you're married. Pregnancy hormones were crazy with Kennedy, but I was convinced there was a demon growing inside of Shannon with baby #2.

When Shannon was in her last month of pregnancy, I admitted to her that she had not been herself this entire pregnancy. She was angry and cranky and downright scary. I was seriously afraid of what was growing inside of her because it made her a different person.

It was a blessing in disguise when she didn't receive that role with her company because it would have been difficult being pregnant and needing to travel a lot, but instead a different role came up a few months later that was a much better fit for our family.

With Shannon's career, we've moved numerous times. It's a confusing timeline so here is the breakdown:

2005: We were married. We both grew up in the Dallas/Fort Worth area in Texas.
2010: We moved to Ocala, Florida.
2013: We moved back to the Dallas/Fort Worth area while Shannon was pregnant with Kennedy.
2015: We moved to Lexington, Kentucky.
2018: We moved to Winter Garden, Florida (outside of Orlando) while Shannon was pregnant with Reagan.

The Clark family can't just have a new baby. With each kid, Shannon started a new role at work, we moved to a new state, and built a new house. Add all of this stress to the pregnancy hormones and taking care of a four year old and life was a bag full of crazy.

The fun was just getting started as we went on our house hunting trip to Orlando. It started with the *worst* travel experience I've ever had.

We waited *six* hours at the airport only to have our flight canceled and be sent back home. My pregnant wife was wondering if this was a sign that we should call it quits and not move to Orlando.

We had to restart the next day and fly to a *different location* way off the grid and *then* to Orlando, missing our initial meeting with the realtor.

On the last day of the last hour of our house hunting trip, we found our dream home that had everything we were looking for. We signed a check and immediately sped to the airport.

We had a layover in Charlotte, North Carolina. Before we even got off the plane, we found out our flight to Lexington had been *canceled*. We effortlessly searched for another flight to *somewhere*. We were put on other flights only to have them canceled *two hours later*.

A regional airline that worked with American Airlines had a computer shut down and nothing was working for the entire weekend. This caused a spiral of issues for all the airlines in many cities, especially across the east coast, causing delays and cancellations all over the country.

We waited for hours to get our bags so we could just stay in Charlotte for the night only to find out that our bags won't be seen and they'll somehow get on a flight back to Lexington without us.

We had to stay in Charlotte overnight and drive the next day. But because we waited so long to get on another flight and then waited for our non-existent bags, I had a matter of minutes to find a store to get a toothbrush and contact solution and the bare essentials we needed to get some rest.

Then, I tried to get something to eat at the restaurant and everyone was there stranded just like us. This was Father's Day and I'm sure the hotel restaurant didn't plan on hundreds of people being stranded late at night. The one bartender and one waitress were trying to take care of everyone. People waited two or more hours for food after all of us were exhausted and many of our families were hangry waiting on us in our hotel rooms.

Chaos upon chaos happened all because of this airline issue.

We drove six hours home the next day instead of flying. The movers were already at our house (with our Godsend of a friend, Mary, monitoring things for us) but certain things we needed since we were going to be in a hotel for 3 months we didn't realize they already packed up until we made it to the hotel.

Then, a few days later, as we jumped in the car to move to Florida, Shannon had an issue with work. She put her hand on my shoulder as a sign of concern. *We weren't moving just yet as we planned.* I was going to be stuck in Kentucky at a hotel with my 4 year old and two dogs *and* all our belongings were on their way to Florida when I could have stayed in our Kentucky home for two more weeks.

Two weeks later we were finally on our car trip to Orlando. Kennedy was sick after a bad experience we had at a restaurant in Atlanta, Georgia. We had a car full of luggage, two dogs, and Shannon pregnant sitting in the back seat with a bucket while Kennedy vomited all the way to Orlando, our new home.

I tell you the story of this chaos and struggle to tell you another story happening at the same time.

//

While we were waiting six hours on that initial trip trying to get out of Lexington, our 4-year old daughter, Kennedy, had one goal: she *needed* one of the pens the American Airline employees had.

She was staring at these pens for a while. She was close to using the force from *Star Wars*[11] to make this pen come to her when Shannon interrupted her force stare.

"Kennedy, you cannot just go up and grab one. You can go ask them *politely* if you can have one," Shannon proclaimed sternly.

Kennedy turned on the charm:

"*May I have a pen please*?", she asked the airline employee.

The cute 4 year old flipped her curly, blonde hair back and smiled sweetly with her Shirley Temple grin. The game was on.

She talked with that employee for a while. By a while, I mean she told her full life story because the door was open for her to talk her head off. The airline employee said, "Here have some extra snacks for waiting so long and here is a sheet for you to color."

Soon the pilots walked up and the airline employee was introducing Kennedy to the pilots and she was telling the pilots her full life story too. And then the pilots gave her a flight book to get signatures from all the pilots she meets on different flights (they must have known all the stupid flights we were about to be on) and Kennedy got multiple airline wings from them.

As other people were angrily getting impatient and some of them yelling at the airline employee, Kennedy was going up to her giving her a hug.

"You made my day so much better!" , the airline employee beamed with joy. And we did too.

Weeks later when Shannon had to go back to Lexington for work, she saw the same employee and she asked how Kennedy was.

A little kindness from a four year old goes a long way when you're under the umbrella of chaos.

//

Five months after we moved to Orlando and two months after we moved into our new home, Reagan made her way into the world.

At first, I wasn't sure if she was going to be the demon she was inside her mommy's belly. But now I can't imagine our lives without her. She made our family of four complete.

She is so different from her sister already. We call her our "serious baby" because she never smiles for professional pictures no matter how hard our photographer, Brittany, tried. If you can catch her candidly, though, she is extra silly and she loves to smile.

My three girls are my entire world and my reason for smiling.

But Scott was right that going from one to two kids is tremendously harder.

Somehow you just get used to the lack of sleep. You're tired all the time but at some point you don't even care anymore.

As a stay-at-home dad, there are times when the 4 month old is asleep during the day and it's complete silence for what seems like a lifetime.

Then there is the "witching hour" when my wife gets home from work and I get home with big sister and the baby at the same time. My wife helps me get the baby out of the car seat but she doesn't notice the baby has had a "blow out." Meaning, well, the diaper didn't do its job.

Now, there is poop all over the car seat, my wife, and the baby. I'm trying to make dinner and help them clean up, my wife is putting the baby in the bath tub, Kennedy, my now 5 year old is trying to put her baby doll in the bathtub too and she starts crying when I tell her to stop, I'm running up and down the stairs to get what my wife needs for the baby, and then I just stop and laugh hysterically.

My body aches all over, I have a twitch in my eye, I had like weird indigestion for the last few days from all the stress of the screaming baby and the craziness, and I've never felt so tired in my life.

Raising tiny humans is the hardest freaking job I've ever had. And I get to do it all again tomorrow.

Everything hurts. But you never stop moving. Dance, piano, laundry, cooking, cleaning, homework, play time, feeding, bath time, brushing your teeth, reading books, "please go to bed," "just watch a show," when *you* finally get to watch a show, you drink bourbon and fall asleep on the couch, and if you try to make love to your spouse the kids wake up immediately.

Catching a break is not synonymous with having kids. You think you're hiring a babysitter to get a date night with your spouse, but the next morning the kids are up at the crack of dawn, that is if you make it to the next morning before they need something.

My motto when you actually get a break from the kids is:

"KIDS DON'T ALLOW HANGOVERS."

It doesn't matter how much fun you had the night before. The next day reality is back and you better be ready. The chaos is coming. They're jumping on your stomach and asking for breakfast and ready to be entertained whether you're ready or not.

Yet you wouldn't trade all this chaos for the world.

The giggles of your little one when you play, "Hug, Kiss, or Tickle?" (They always choose tickle.)
The notes that say "I love you Daddy."
The girls showing glimpses of being like you (in a good way).
The girls taking an interest in something you like.
Sometimes they sleep and you remember how lucky you are.
Sometimes they do something sweet for others and you get to witness it.

The next second they might be smothering their sister, but then they make each other laugh so hard that your heart jumps out of your chest. When teachers tell you your kids are the "helper" in class and "they're so friendly," then you think "*maybe we're doing something right.*"

At first the chaos of raising kids throws you off balance, but then the chaos *is* your balance. You welcome it. You wouldn't know what to do without it. It's your life now.

These crazy girls keep us living.

//

I still remember my 3rd grade teacher said that one day I would be president. Instead, I became a minister, and now a stay-at-home dad. I called Reagan my "job security" for continuing to be a stay-at-home dad.

When Shannon and I were talking about what to name baby #2, we both decided upon Reagan quickly because we liked the name. I asked Shannon, "We already have a Kennedy. Do we really want a Reagan, another president's name?"

"I don't care. Do you?" She replied.

"No, I like the name."

"Me too."

It is fitting too for us to have both Democrat and Republican presidential names since Shannon and I vote differently. I think our difference in politics in our marriage has brought a balance to the way we think and react to others and to how we parent are very different children.

Shannon's friend asked her if we were naming our kids after airports, you know, the Ronald Reagan airport and the John F. Kennedy airport.

Face. Palm.

"No, we're naming them after the presidents, Kennedy and Reagan, who the airports are named after...but it's really just because we like the names," Shannon replied kindly.

So, no, we're not raising airports. And I'm pretty sure I won't be president one day like my 3rd grade teacher predicted.

But we are – in fact – *raising presidents*.

Chapter 4
The Stay-at-Home Dad: Parenting is Not Just for Moms

"Tell them in your job interview that you've been a stay-at-home dad for the last three years. That makes you a f------ superhero! You're not, but they don't know that." – from Catastrophe *on Amazon Prime Video* [12]

My very first paycheck came from working at a daycare. It was the Mother's Day Out program where my mom worked. Most of my jobs throughout my lifetime have been caring for kids. I was babysitting often for neighborhood kids as soon as I was old enough to do so. My mom was always watching my nephews and nieces or other kids from the Mother's Day Out daycare. There were always kids at my house.

I worked in a very busy pharmacy for almost 5 years throughout high school and part of college. It was one of the few jobs I've had that didn't involve dealing with kids. But it definitely taught me how to deal with stress. It helped me prepare for the chaos of raising sick and cranky and hangry kids and balancing multiple tasks at once. When someone was sick and they were upset with their doctor or insurance or the pharmacist, they took it out on me. This highly stressful job taught me to stay calm while others were screaming around you and amidst this chaos recognizing the responsibility of making sure the right prescription made it to the right person.

All I wanted to be after high school was a youth minister. I wanted kids and teens to have the same experience at church that I did. As I got older, I learned that kids and teens were often ignored in the church. I had a very positive experience at church as a teenager, but I soon learned this was not the case for the majority of teenagers. The sermons never related to them. Church was "boring" and church people were judgmental and the messages received were not relevant to their lives. I had a problem with this being the perception my peers had of church.

When I became a pastor, one of the moms said, "My 5th grader was asking me questions about your sermon that I didn't have the answer to, but do you know what that means?! My *5th grader* was listening to your sermon!"

One elderly member said, "The kids are listening to your sermon! You've made something they can relate to!"

I leaned in close to her and said, *"Guess what? You deserve a message that won't put you to sleep too!"*

My time as a pastor prepared me for my future role as a parent. All of my previous jobs have prepared me to be a dad in some way. Caring for children and delivering a meaningful message has always been a central role of my life and career and calling.

When I was about to become a stay-at-home dad, my pastor colleagues insisted this would be the time of my life staying home with my daughter. I didn't know just how much I would treasure it.

I had the time of my life as a pastor, but when Kennedy was born it was time to fulfill my destiny.

//

I think hearing the voice of God is weird. I'm not saying it doesn't happen and everyone's experience is different, but even as a pastor I was uncomfortable with the idea of hearing a voice from the clouds. As a teenager, I felt like God spoke through my friends at church often. The few times I felt like God actually spoke to me was in college.

One of the times God spoke to me I heard "she's the one" and I knew then Shannon was going to be my wife.

God also told me I was destined to be a dad.

I've always felt like being a dad was my destiny but I never knew just how pivotal of a role it would become in my life.

//

"You trust him to watch the baby?", Shannon's friend asked when she returned to work from maternity leave.

"Actually," Shannon replied, "He does a better job with her than I do. He is so patient with her that I trust him completely."

Shannon and I knew when we moved back to Texas to be around family that I would be a stay-at-home dad for a while. We knew I wasn't going to have a pastoral appointment for a while; we just didn't know it was *indefinitely*.

Shannon couldn't believe her friend had this reaction. When she told me what her friend said, she knew it would upset me.

"Dads aren't capable of taking care of their own children?!" I snapped back.

I don't think either one of us knew the gravity of the decision we made compared to society's typical gender roles.

For us, it was a no-brainer. Shannon has been very successful in her career, providing for our family much better than my full-time work/part-time salary as a pastor.

I am 38 years old today. It's now been 7 years since I left the ministry and became a stay-at-home dad. I have technically *never* had a full-time job. I've had full-time work all my life and gone above and beyond what's required of me but it's weird to say I've never had a full-time job. As a youth minister, I worked crazy hours, especially during the summer. As a pastor, I was on call 24/7 and I often worked 60 hours a week but I worked for a small church so I was declared "part-time." As a father now, I'm always at work but these kids have the *nerve* not to pay me a dime!

But if I were a stay-at-home mom and woman this would be more "normal." I often feel like I need to defend myself for being a stay-at-home dad because being a man is synonymous with working. I know stay-at-home moms have had to defend their decision to stay home with the children too.

Shannon often feels the same way about defending her choice to be the working mom and breadwinner.

When we saw a now *former* friend write a blog saying that the problem with society is more men are staying home and more women are working, we were taken aback.

She said, "God intends for a man's job to be at work and a woman's job is to be at home to take care of the family. Anything different is *less than* what God intended."

"Wow…" was my reaction when Shannon shared that with me. "We are *less than*."

With a look of shock, Shannon confessed to me how she felt about our friend's blog: "I can't look at their lives and their children the same knowing they think less of us because of what we have decided to do with our careers and our family. I don't want to see them anymore and be reminded of that when it's hard enough to be a working mother and working *woman* in a 'man's workforce'. I don't need to see things like this."

We decided to completely remove this family from our lives – as much as we once loved them (and truthfully still do) – because we feel confident in how we have redefined gender roles. *And we are damn good at it!*

Don't let anyone call you "less than" when you're doing what is best for yourself and your family! There is nothing more important than living out your unique, individual God-given purpose and caring for your family!

Being confident as a stay-at-home dad was one of the first and most important lessons I learned in my new role.

"If I am going to do this, I need to invest myself 110%. I'm going to be the best at packing that damn diaper bag! I'm going to rock fixing my daughter's pigtails! The world will see what I do and know this dad is just as good – or better – than stay-at-home moms!"

//

Yet, being a stay-at-home dad is lonely because it is so unusual to our society's standards. It was really hard at the beginning because it was hard to find any fellow stay-at-home dads.

When you're at-home with a newborn who doesn't talk and doesn't move much but only communicates by screams and coos and dirty diapers, the loneliness sets in quickly. All my family and friends were busy with their own lives and I quickly learned this new job was up to me to figure out. I *longed* for adult conversation.

Not to mention, I was grieving the loss of my career and trying to navigate those emotions. I was really depressed both at how my career ended and I lost many friends who were colleagues when I left the ministry. I eventually buried those emotions for years because I was solely focused on caring for my daughter. She was my utmost joy carrying me through that time.

Kennedy and I enjoyed our trips to the grocery stores and the zoo. We found a "mommy and me" playtime at the recreation center where I felt really out of place as a dad with all the breastfeeding moms. They had their mom friends they were meeting up with and it was uncomfortable for most of them to talk to the dad. I gravitated towards the grandmas so I didn't appear to be flirting with the moms – and the grandmas were the most comfortable talking to me. My daughter eventually became the social butterfly and she made it easier to break the ice with other parents.

But at first, the loneliness and depression were real. The quiet moments of the day were so quiet they were deafening.

One day I actually drove around with the baby determined that we were going to do something fun. I thought about eating out but since the baby had me up at the crack of dawn it was still too early to eat at a restaurant. I went to an outlet mall and walked around with the baby in her stroller thinking about all the possible places we could go to or eat at. Then it was the baby's nap time so we drove back home and I ate leftovers from the refrigerator. Stay-at-home life is really exciting.

When I would get a night out with friends, all the guys were talking about their work and I would reply, "Well, Kennedy ate most of her lunch, had two poopy diapers and four wet diapers today, and we watched the same episode of *Paw Patrol*[13] twenty times."

Staying at home now with Reagan I'm reminded of all the emotion I felt the first time around. I was reminded of how lonely and depressed I really was. I didn't know then what I know now. Back then I thought I was alone in this, I felt ashamed for not being a working dad, and I felt a lack of purpose after being a pastor serving a congregation and "making a difference in the world."

I learned that this loneliness and depression are actually really common among stay-at-home parents.

Taking care of your mental health is important as a stay-at-home parent. I am no expert on dealing with depression and loneliness, but what I do have is my personal experience. What has helped me is to go outside and be around other people, even if it's awkward being the only dad. Just being around people and being outdoors is healthy for you and your kids.

You also need to take breaks from your kids. We love our kids but we can't be the best for our kids if we don't also take care of ourselves. Take them to the grandparent's house or hire a babysitter. It is ok to send them to daycare too for you to have time to recharge. It's also okay to put their favorite show on so you can do what you need to do.

You need to find something you love to do away from your kids – to find both a sense of purpose and to get a mental health break from loud kids shows and even louder kids screaming. Sometimes this can be as simple as watching a show you like or reading a book or taking a nap when the baby naps.

After four years of being a stay-at-home dad, I realized I never fully allowed myself to come to terms with ending my career and becoming a stay-at-home parent. Don't wait that long to process your current situation. Counseling helped me by reminding me who I am (and who I am not).

It helped me address the negative voices in my head and the situations out of my control so I could stand up and be myself again. It gave me the sense of purpose again to write my first book, *Loser*, and do something I love. The bottom line: don't be afraid to talk to a mental health professional. You're worth it.

And find a safe place to vent your frustrations. Don't post your frustrations on social media unless you want unwarranted advice or older parents saying, "But some day you'll miss this!" *Shut up, Karen! No one asked you!*

//

I found my people in the "Brotherhood of Fatherhood" of The National At-Home Dad Network. These guys have saved me in many ways. I attended my first At-Home Dad Convention in September 2018 and it's so great to know other dads who are "dadding" just like me. The National At-Home Dad Network's goal is to provide "advocacy, education, community, and support." [14]

It's important to know we're not alone in this.

In our network, we can share our frustrations when restaurants don't have baby changing tables in their restrooms and ask for advice without fear of being insulted for doing a "woman's job." We can share how pissed off we are with how dads are portrayed in film, television, and commercials. We can support each other when we are going through a difficult time with the kids and our families. We can educate new dads on how to balance the daily activities or the loneliness of being a stay-at-home parent. We can be advocates for each other and LGBT dads and Black dads when we need to be lifted up and supported in our communities. We can find that connection with other dads that is essential to our success and our mental health.

As part of The National At-Home Dad Network and other dads groups, we are breaking barriers of what a dad is on a daily basis. Now I proudly share that this is my job and my purpose. What I did as a pastor to empower people and help them believe in themselves and be who God made them to be and to be loving and kind to all people – especially outcasts, I now get to teach to my two daughters. I moved from a macro-congregation to my micro-family. I get to embody for my family what I taught my congregation as a pastor. I get to fully embrace with confidence my departure from the traditional male role.

But being a stay-at-home dad is still not the norm in many circles.

We have all received comments such as:

"How's motherhood?"
"Are you still playing Mr. Mom?"
"You know how to change a diaper? That's neat when dads can change diapers."
"You're such a great cook. You'll make a great wife someday."
"Are you doing the mommy duties today?"
"When are you going to get a real job?"
"But how do you know what to do when the kids are sick when you don't have motherly instincts?"
"Is daddy babysitting today?"

As The National At-Home Dad Network slogan goes:

"Dads don't babysit. It's called *parenting*."

I usually fix my daughter's hair every day. If we're out in public and her hair looks great I get, "Oh, mom did a great job fixing her hair today!" And I say, "No, daddy fixes her hair every day." If she has a bad hair day, I get, "Oh, *daddy* fixed her hair today..." I'm like, "I fix her hair every day dammit and today was a rough day so give me a break!"

The most insulting comments I've ever had, though, came from a mortgage consultant.

When Shannon and I were moving to Kentucky in 2015, the mortgage consultant asked what Shannon and I do for a living and we each told him. When I said I'm a stay-at-home dad, Shannon quickly said, *"And he works harder than I ever do!",* upon which the mortgage consultant laughed in my face.

My body language quickly switched from smiling to pissed off.

Strike one.

Then, he asked what neighborhood we were looking to move into. Shannon told him what area we were looking at because I had already shut down from this meeting. His reply was, *"If you move into my neighborhood, you can babysit my kids too!"*

Strike two.

For whatever reason, we were still sitting in this consultation. He then had the nerve to tell me, "You know, your name doesn't even need to be on this mortgage because *you don't make any money.* This mortgage is only debt and since you don't have a job your name doesn't need to be on it."

Strike three.

Needless to say, we didn't get our mortgage at that bank.

People like this mortgage consultant are the reason the dads at The National At-Home Dad Network are so passionate about what we do. We're redefining what a dad's role is and showing the world this is our full-time job. We are *very* proud of the work we do as dads. We are involved in our kids schools. We are active in our communities. We have created dad groups in our own cities to provide support and comradery. Many of us have side gigs to either make some extra money for our families or simply to do something that we love but all of us would agree that our job as dads is our first priority – and it's a lifetime commitment.

//

A common challenge many of the stay-at-home dads have faced is how everything having to do with parenting is only geared towards moms. Parenting magazines and Parenting Facebook groups might as well be called Mom groups. I'm constantly changing quotes and memes that mention how hard it is to be a mom to include dads too. When they talk about how hard it is to keep the house clean as a mom, I'm like, "I do that too!" When they talk about how stressful and lonely it is as a mom, I'm like, "I'm with you!" Then they bad-mouth their husbands and the father of their children for not being involved, and I'm like, *"Actually, my wife is dying to get home from work to help out and spend time with the kids."*

I once was talking with a group of moms and mentioned how tired I was and she said, "Oh, you poor baby..." mockingly. I was deeply offended because I have the same job of taking care of the kids and balancing everyone's schedules and cleaning the house and cooking the meals and getting the kids to bed just like these moms. But then I considered the source. This mom didn't have a husband who was active to care for her and the kids.

The truth is moms have a right to complain. While I get upset at the lack of inclusion of dads in parenting groups, the truth is I'm the minority. For my wife and me, we know parenting is both of our jobs, even though I'm a stay-at-home dad. For the families where both parents work or the mom stays at home and the dad works, the mom is considered the go-to parent. The dad isn't the active father he should be. He relies completely on the mom to be the parent, the maid, the chauffer, the chef, the finance manager, the budget planner, the party planner, the schedule keeper, the school liaison, and the domestic CEO.

It upsets us stay-at-home dads when dads don't get the respect they deserve, but then we look at other dads outside of our group and we're like, "Well, maybe they have a point."

See, dads get credit when we just show up. Moms have to be the Pinterest mom, the fit and healthy mom who makes fit and healthy meals for the kids, the designer mom who has the kids looking like fashion models and their projects have to be something that goes viral.

Dads can put the kids pants on and stick a meal in the microwave and we're great dads.

When the movies *Bad Moms* [15] and *Bad Moms 2* [16] came out, the actresses in the film said in an interview that this movie is for all moms because being a mom is hard. It's for all the moms to know that they're doing great even when the expectations for being a mom are so high in today's world. I know mom guilt is a thing. I see it with my wife often (even though she is awesome and shouldn't ever feel this way).

As much as I hate to admit it because I like to think I can do everything a mom can do being a stay-at-home dad, there are still things my wife is so much better at as a parent than me. It's just our different gifts that make us both needed to complete the picture for our daughters, even when we are breaking stereotypes every day of what a mom and dad can do.

This led me to think, "What would a movie like this look like for dads" Would it be called "Good Dads"? Would it be a movie to show a lot of dads who are active in their kid's lives? We can fix our daughter's hair. We can be capable to be left alone with our children for an hour, a day, a week alone. While moms are stressed out to meet expectations, dads know that if we give our kids a high five we met society's expectations.

Moms have to be exceptional; dads have to show up to be praised.

The difference between moms and dads is expectations. Moms need to be cut some slack – working mom or not. They need some appreciation for what they do – because they're awesome. Dads – on the other hand – need to step it up. What I'm trying to change and what the stay-at-home dads and active fathers I know are trying to change is this: we're parents too. It's our job to change dirty diapers and get up in the middle of the night and to help cook and clean and to raise the expectations of what being a dad looks like.

I know so many dads who are really there for their kids – stay-at-home dad or not. Maybe we need to know good dads exist.

Good dads, we need to keep raising the bar.

Bad moms, keep doing your thing.

I get it that some moms get frustrated with their spouses because they don't do a thing to help with the kids or help with cooking and cleaning. It's those dads that need to "man up" and understand just how hard this job is! It should never be one person's responsibility to care for *your* home and *your* child!

Let me say it louder for the people in the back: *It's not a woman's job to cook and clean and care for the children.*

There's a lot of talk about masculinity today and redefining what that looks like. As the dad of two daughters, the way I feel is being a dad who dresses up and plays with blocks and plays hide 'n' seek *and* who also loves my wife unconditionally and respects her and gives her mommy time *is the most masculine thing I can do*. I can show my two daughters what a real partner looks like so they know how they should be treated if they choose to look for a future spouse and father to their children. (More on this later.)

Being a dad is my most important job. It is my greatest responsibility. It makes me more of a man than any power I could have or money I could make. Being a dad is making the greatest impact I could ever make in this world. Loving my girls and nurturing and caring for them and empowering them to be awesome is not "mom's job."

It's a parent's job.

And parenting should always include dads.

The voice of God once told me *it's our destiny.*

Chapter 5
The Working Mom: A Mother's Sacrifice

"I'm going to be staying home with my baby on my own for the first time tomorrow when my wife goes back to work," a fellow stay-at-home dad messaged me. "What advice can you give me?"

*My response: "Send your wife lots of pictures and encourage her. **It's harder on the working mom than it is on us.**"*

Shannon has had just as much of a tough time being a working mom as I have being a stay-at-home dad.

She struggled to make time for the girls when she is exhausted after work.
She has felt "mom guilt" for not being able to be home when Kennedy is sick even

though she knows I am fully capable of caring for her.

She has struggled with working long hours and going on work trips and still wanting to be fully present at home.

And she feels the need to help me because she just wants to be involved (not because she thinks I can't do my job at home).

This really annoyed me at first because I felt like she was telling me I wasn't doing a good enough job, but then she made me aware that it was more about dealing with her mom guilt for not being home. When we've taken on these new roles, I wanted to feel confident being a stay-at-home dad and she wanted to know she wasn't a failure as a mom. We both had to come to grips with allowing each other to take on our new roles.

Shannon gets really annoyed when people say how great of a dad I am because I am coloring the sidewalk with chalk with the kids or I am taking the kids on an adventure or I'm playing dress-up with them. It's not that she's not really proud of what I do and loves that I'm an active father; it's that it's only because she's a hard-working mom that I'm able to do my job at home. And she's a super mom too! But they don't always see what she does or get amazed by it because moms are expected to be that way.

I asked Shannon what it feels like to be a working mom:

"When I'm at work, I feel guilty I'm not with the kids.
When I'm at home with the kids, I feel guilty I'm not doing more at work.
When I'm on a date with you, you want a break from the kids but I feel guilty I'm not with them.
It's mom guilt no matter what I do."

Shannon is now in a leadership position in her career. She is one step away from being a director. To say I'm proud of her would be an understatement. She deserves every penny and every inkling of respect she has earned because she's the smartest person and the hardest worker I know. She doesn't give up until she gets what she wants. (Trust me. I've learned after 15 years of marriage that she will *always* get what she wants.) Her aspirations and her goals become a reality because she will do what needs to be done to be successful.

When I first met Shannon, what attracted me to her first was how independent she was. I loved my "crazy business lady." As a minister, some girls I dated needed me for advice or guidance but Shannon didn't need me. She had such a strong head on her shoulders and I've always loved that about her. I loved that she didn't need me; she *wanted* me.

The Board of Ordained Ministry in The United Methodist Church always had a problem with me choosing my wife's career over my own. As a pastor, I was supposed to commit myself fully to the church and promise to go wherever they send me. But when Shannon feared what this meant for her career I told her, "God comes first, our family second, and the church third. If something comes up for your career or my own, we'll talk about what is best for our family first."

This division with what the church expected of me eventually lead me to choose to be a stay-at-home dad for the last seven years. I left ministry and never looked back. And we've moved multiple times to help Shannon's career because *my male career did not trump our marriage and doing what's best for our family.*

At a work Christmas party Shannon had, I quickly learned that at her company many of the spouses were stay-at-home parents. She has a very demanding, time-consuming career and it is really common for spouses from her company to be stay-at-home parents.

Shannon and I every so often do a check-up of the abnormal roles we have taken on of stay-at-home dad and working mom, and after a brief examination we realize what we are doing really works and we couldn't imagine doing life together any other way.

We're raising presidents – or business women or CEOs or teachers or artists or actresses or engineers or stay-at-home parents – but whatever our kids become they will know they can be whoever they want to be because they've watched one, powerful, hard-working mama in action their entire lives.

Shannon told me about a study that says girls who have stay-at-home dads are more likely to become successful business women because they have dads who teach them to be strong and independent and they see what it's like to have a mother who is strong and successful.

I've watched Kennedy and Reagan both learn to be more independent. At the playground, I've given them space to try new things and attempt to be daredevils. Sometimes they fall and skin their knee but I never feed into their tantrums – and because of this they throw less tantrums and they've become stronger because of it.

I might be the one at home, but we're *both* raising strong, independent women just like mommy. I couldn't be such a "great dad" like people love to say when they see me spending time with the kids if it weren't for the amazing, hard-working mom she is. She keeps this ship sailing and she keeps this family strong. I know we'll raise some super Wonder Women because they'll see the strongest Wonder Woman is our working mama.

//

When Shannon went back to work for the first time after her maternity leave, I knew that my first day at home with the baby is not the hard part; it's mommy's first day back at work. A newborn sleeps a lot and the hardest part for an at-home parent is the deafening quiet moments. The working parent has to deal with the need to be at work but strongly wanting to be at home every second of the day. I try to send mommy pictures and updates and stories often so when she gets a break she can know she's included and loved and thought of and that everything is okay at home until she gets back.

My job is just as much about raising tough, kind girls as it is about supporting my wife.

My wife certainly needs "mommy breaks" because she is worn out by the time she makes it home from a long day at work, but she makes a complete effort to be present for our daughters when she is home. She doesn't expect me to be the only one to help with the children or take care of the house because she knows I need help sometimes. Typically, I make her sit down and relax when she gets home because some days are easier for me than they are for her. I cook and clean the dishes and get the kids ready for bed on most days because she needs that time to chill when she gets home. But she is still there to be an active parent and spouse when we need her.

By the way, she is a freaking bolt of lightning when it comes to changing out of her work clothes into her pajamas. I hardly ever see her in her work clothes before she is in her pajamas the next second. Superman could never change in the phone booth as fast as my wife does after work.

Also, moms, I have something important to say to you as a stay-at-home dad about "mommy breaks": *Don't be afraid to go out and leave your kids at home with dad.* Stay-at-home parent or not. Working parent or not. We all need a break from our kids and each parent is fully capable of caring for their kids alone. Parenting is really friggin' hard and parents need to care for themselves so they can care for their families. You need a break. Your spouse needs to give you a break. Both spouses need to give each other a break from their kids. And you both need time together away from your kids. Period.

//

Shannon and I are definitely not perfect when it comes to parenting. We're just as stressed with the mess as everyone else. But parenting and marriage means we are present for one another and we have conversations daily about what our needs are. We are constantly learning how to be a better team.

We both work hard to make sure our family is taken care of, our marriage needs are communicated, and our individual needs are met.

We both have defined our individual and family purpose and what we believe God intends for us to do at this time in our lives.

It's important for spouses to sit down and define what their expectations are from the beginning when it comes to parenting. It starts during pregnancy. The amount of time I spent supporting Shannon during her pregnancy giving her foot massages and doing late night Taco Bell runs and encouraging her when she didn't feel like herself reflected directly with how active I would become as a father. Dads need to start training themselves from pregnancy to birth of what kind of dad they will become. Go to the doctor's appointments and read the books on becoming a dad and get the hospital bag ready to go. Show immediately how active of a father you will be because – working dad or not – we should all be active fathers.

//

Shannon and I are different than some couples because we are both very organized and very OCD when it comes to a clean house. Friends have called our home a model home because it's always in order. It didn't help that both times we moved into a new home Shannon was pregnant and nesting. I ran myself ragged getting our home in order before we had each girl because I had a pregnant woman with pizza in one hand and a proverbial whip in the other hand making sure our house was ready before the baby arrived.

Since I was a little kid, my mind feels free when my house is clean and organized. I know. I'm weird. But being a stay-at-home dad has been the greatest challenge for an OCD person to keep my house in order with two crazy kids. I plan out a menu and grocery list on my phone each week so I know what we'll have for dinner each day and we don't waste produce I've purchased. I try to stick to certain chores each day so when the weekend rolls around Shannon and I can both spend time with each other and our girls without having to worry about getting groceries or cleaning the house. It doesn't always work out this way, but having a plan and trying to stick with it helps keep our sanity.

Staying organized – both with our schedules and keeping a clean home – makes us happy and I recognize that every family is different and we're all doing what works for our individual families to stay happy, healthy, and somewhat sane.

When I was a kid, I never imagined this would be the role I would take on. I didn't grow up dreaming of fixing girls hair every day or being the primary cook. When I met Shannon, I thought you warmed up spaghetti sauce by putting the jar in the microwave and almost set her apartment on fire!

Now I love cooking. I love preparing a menu and cooking a new meal from Pinterest and grilling is a passion of mine. Cooking and cleaning and getting the kids ready for school and other activities are my responsibility – my job – and I take the work that I do very seriously and with the utmost passion. If my job lifts my wife up so she can do her job and our family is taken care of, then I am proud to be the Trophy Husband and Domestic CEO.

//

When I was a minister, I would put Shannon to sleep talking about my job constantly. My time as a pastor taught me how to be a better husband. Now I understand the importance of giving my wife time to debrief from her hard day at work. Now I'm able to make things easier on her by doing my best to prepare a home-cooked meal, clean the house, have the kids ready for bed, and have them ready for school the next day.

Like I said, this doesn't always happen and Shannon knows how tough my day is with crying kids and taking them to different activities, but when I can't get everything done we set expectations of what we hope can be completed first.

As I mentioned earlier, the worst time every day for any parent is "The Witching Hour." This is when I'm getting the kids home from school and they're hangry and screaming and laying out their requests and I'm trying to prepare dinner and Shannon is calling me wanting to debrief her day and I just can't because of everything I have going on in the background.

On some days, I tell her I just can't talk right now because it's bat sh*t crazy in the house. On some days, she knows I need a break immediately before she walks in the door. On other days, I know to drop everything because she needs a listening ear on the way home. The point is we understand what's happening in our different worlds and we seek to meet our needs and the needs of our children that are different on any given day.

//

What is most important for my working mom to know is *we appreciate you.*

Every time I share a cute photo of me and the kids doing something fun, what you can't see in every photo is Shannon is hard at work being the breadwinner for our family.

Every time someone says, "What a great dad you are," it's because of the sacrifice mommy is making every day.

When moms share cute photos, moms are just doing their thing.
But when dads do it, it's special.

What's actually special is mommy has worked over 12 hours many days to be the best at her job.

What's actually special is she swiftly changes into her pajamas when she gets home and changes from super working woman to super attentive mom.

Let me be clear: the only reason I can do what I do is because of what she does. And the only reason she can do the work she does is because of what I do.

We're a team.

We've been doing this for 7 years now and we love what we do. It's tough at times, for sure, but we make it work the best we can. You might not see one of us in all the cute photos, but *she's always there*. I'm a "great dad" because of an even better mommy who comes up with the crafts, stays awake at night thinking of activities for the kids and ways to make them feel special and loved, and takes the crying kids after a long day because mommy's work isn't done when her work day is over. She's our superhero that paves the way for our kids to go on adventures daily.

We love you Mommy and we're so proud of you!

Your sacrifice never goes unnoticed.

To the moms
by Russell Clark
11/7/16

To all the hard-working ladies, especially my wife, Shannon.
To the get up early, stay up late, can't go to sleep ladies,
To the master degrees, follow your dreams, rise to the top ladies,
To the making a difference, lending a helping hand, going the extra mile ladies,
To the time managing, feel guilty for taking 5 minutes for yourself ladies,
To the beautiful inside and out, this bra is killing me, who created these damn heels ladies (and I repeat you're beautiful),
To the strong, determined, take no crap ladies,
To the work 12 hours and still make dance class ladies,
To the working mom, dropping everything to hug your child, still caring for all of us when we are sick ladies,
To the women who don't need a man to define who you are, or to be submissive for, but the men in your life complement you and lift you up for you being you ladies,

Don't let anyone in this world tell you that you can't be anything you want to be,
Don't let anyone tell you men are programmed differently and women can't do what a man can do and do it better,
Don't let anyone make you hide behind the man in your life,
Don't let anyone use a vagina as a derogatory, put-you-down kind of term, but be proud of who you are and all that you do (because you do more than you think you do).

Real men won't be threatened by you but will cheer you on because they want what's best for the women in their life,
And we know God is still creating a world where we all are beautiful and diverse and different and we don't have to be who others tell us to be but we can be anyone we want to be because God created us all to be awesome!

Be empowered because you empower us.
And we love you, superheroes.

Love,
Your sons, brothers, fathers, husbands

Chapter 6
Longing for the Moments

"You're not just anyone. One day you're going to make a choice. You have to decide what kind of man you want to grow up to be. Whoever that man is – good character or bad – is going to change the world." – Jonathan Kent to Clark Kent (Superman) as a young boy in Man of Steel[17]

When Shannon had her miscarriages and it seemed like we would never be parents, I remember rocking my niece, Reese, to sleep. Chad and Kacie – her parents – were on vacation visiting us and they were becoming increasingly frustrated with her unwillingness to go to sleep. I offered to take her. I took her to the back porch and rocked her and held her tight while she screamed bloody murder.

Kacie checked on me a few times and I whispered, "Don't worry. I got this."

She was a stubborn, rotten baby who put up a good fight that night. But I continued to rock her and whisper to her and patiently waited for her to fall asleep. I began to pray about being a dad and acknowledged the pain I had felt of not being able to become one at that time.

She finally gave up. She laid there in my arms with her sweet eyes closed and I began to sob uncontrollably.

I didn't know that one year and one month later my prayers would finally be answered when I became a dad for the first time.

//

My best friend of 19 years, Richard, also felt this pain of longing to be a father but having it stripped away.

He was dating a mutual friend in 2015 – and they hit it off immediately. She became pregnant after dating a few months. He was preparing to be a stay-at-home dad to his pregnant girlfriend and her two boys from previous relationships. But when she became angry one day, she made some comments that he felt were unforgivable.

They were planning to move for her career, but after they broke up these plans changed. She stayed home to be with her family to help raise her two boys. And Richard entered into a deep depression because of what happened next.

"She told me, *'This baby isn't good for my life and I'm going to end it.'*"

"What did you say?" I asked.

"I told her I will take the baby and give her money if she will just keep the baby."

I asked my sister, Tina, who is a lawyer, if he has any rights as the unborn baby's father:

"Unfortunately, the mother has all the rights to the unborn child. A father has no say about his rights to the child until after the baby is born."

It was August 2015 at Kennedy's 2nd birthday party when I remember giving Richard a big hug because he was preparing to tell his parents the news that they were not going to become grandparents after all.

//

Two years later, another long-time friend, Aaron, was getting married back in Texas. I flew down for his wedding to be the DJ. I had large speakers I borrowed from his church in my parent's van for the wedding the next day. Shannon convinced me not to leave the speakers in the vehicle overnight because it wasn't safe and I'd be held responsible if anything happened.

So, I called another friend who lived close to my parents. He helped me unload the speakers and then we popped open a few beers and started catching up. He told me he and his wife had recently started attending a church I used to work at. I said, "Oh yeah. We have an old friend who attends that church too. Funny story. She was supposed to have a baby with Richard, but she decided to not have the baby a couple years ago after they broke up."

He sat back in his chair and squinted his eyes.

"Well, you know my wife and I share a Facebook page and we're friends with this girl on Facebook. My wife told me the other day that she saw something weird from her. One day she said she was pregnant. The next day she said she had a baby. Then the next day the baby was 3 months old and then the next day 6 months and then the next day a year old. She called it her 'Secret Baby.'"

I sat back in my chair and squinted my eyes.

"HOLY SH*T!" we both screamed out.

"Holy sh*t! My best friend has a kid out there and he doesn't know it! She tried to hide the baby from him?! Who does that?! How did she think she would ever get away with this?! Who the f--- does that?!"

I had to call Richard and tell him he has a daughter he doesn't know about it. She never had the abortion and didn't tell him.

Just breathe. I'll give you a minute.

At first, Richard was in shock. Then he was excited to know he had a daughter. Then he was overcome with anger that this woman could be so disgusting to keep his own daughter from him and not even share that she existed.

//

Calli was born in February 2016.

Richard met his daughter for the first time on August 24, 2017, when she was 1.5 years old. A day that changed his life and his heart forever.

Before Calli, Richard had been through a deep, crippling depression thinking that he could have been a dad but that was stripped away. He was in the middle of becoming a minimalist and selling off most of his possessions. I'm not sure he felt much purpose in his life anymore.

But August 24, 2017 gave my friend new life and a new joy I had never seen in him before.

Richard visited me in Florida in March 2020 when Calli was 4. Reagan was 15 months old at the time. Calli was 18 months old when Richard met her. It just killed me and still kills me that Richard lost the first 18 months of her life.

Richard was robbed of seeing her as a newborn. He was robbed of getting to help decide her name – *his own daughter's name*! (Her actual name is Calliope, but when she is with Richard's family and friends, we call her Calli.) He didn't get to see her first steps or first words or anything first-time parents get the joy of experiencing.

He was scared to put her in the car seat the first time he had her because he didn't know kids always scream when you put them in their car seat. He was so frightened when he first became a dad and he called me often for advice. I loved to see my friend blossom into the dedicated dad he is now.

It wasn't long before he was totally smitten with his daughter. She is the center of his world. He gets so excited about teaching her new things and laughing with her and taking her places.

What he lost the first 18 months with her, he has made up that time with her by leaps and bounds.

Richard said he calculated for the 2019-2020 school year (including the summer) he gets 98 days total with Calli. That's 26% of the year he is with his daughter.

Just the fact that he made that calculation shows anyone how much he longs to be with his daughter.

It kills Richard that he has such limited time with her. One day he was preparing to take her back to her mom's house when Calli picked up a big book to read.

"Daddy, will you please read this book to me?"

"Calli, we don't have time to read a long book right now."

Richard said he teared up a little bit that he had to say that to her.

If you could see the love these two have for each other and the way they make the most of every second they have together, it would inspire all of us to be better fathers and better parents.

It would inspire us all to make the best of each, little moment because Richard longs every time for the next moment he is reunited with his daughter's embrace.

//

Tina became Richard's lawyer for his custody hearing in 2017. I was in Texas the first time they all went before a judge. The judge immediately pre-judged Richard as some deadbeat dad who wanted nothing to do with his daughter's life until now.

"Why now?! Why are you coming before me now when you weren't involved in this child's life before today?" the judge barked at Richard.

"Judge, I would ask you not to assume things about my client until all the details of his case are able to come forward." I remember my sister responding.

Richard received the same, standard custody as many dads in Texas. He gets every Wednesday evening with her and he gets the 1st, 3rd, and 5th weekends – and if a holiday or spring break falls on his weekend then he gets her for that extra day/week. And he gets her for one month during the summer.

Dads all over the country have had to fight for custody of their children. Some of my stay-at-home dad friends have been fighting to give dads in their respective states equal rights for custody.

Dads of the past wouldn't have fought for custody.
Dads of the past wouldn't have even searched for their long-lost child.
Dads of the past wouldn't have longed to be full-time dads. They would have been satisfied being average dads. They would have been declared successful being moderately present.

Dads of yesterday wouldn't have longed to be a dad.
Dads of yesteryear wouldn't have longed for more time.

But many dads today don't equate success with money and power. Many of us equate success with the impact we've had raising our children and caring for our families.

We're more than a paycheck or child support and the occasional lap talk.

We're on the ground reading to our kids. We're cleaning up boo boos and showing we have fatherly instincts when our kids are in distress. We're making healthy meals and healthy decisions for our kids to become successful individuals.

We're not defined by power, but becoming completely powerless to a little girl in a tutu who calls us "Daddy."

Our success is defined in the sparkle of that little girl's eyes.

Our masculinity, our embodiment of our manhood, is defined in longing and fighting and making the most of the moments we have with our children.

Fatherhood is our top priority.
Being a dad is our most important job.

//

I've actually only had two visits with Calli. I met her at my parent's house in March 2019 and I fell in love instantly.

Then in March 2020 we were all able to go to Disneyworld together for a few days. It was great to have my friend here, and see our daughters become friends like we have been for years.

This was only a week before we were all quarantined in our homes due to the Coronavirus. It was serendipitous that we were able to go to "The Happiest Place on Earth" together before we were all stuck in our homes and Disneyworld ended up closing for 4 months.

I could just freeze that moment in time when Richard had unicorn Mickey ears on because Calli didn't want to wear them and she was asleep on his shoulders from being "Disney-tired" at the end of the most magical day.

This magical moment between a dad and his daughter was made possible because I just happened to be in town for a wedding and I decided to have a beer with a friend.

Dads long for these moments.
We should fight for dads to have these moments.

Chapter 7
Feminist Father: My Future is Female

Kennedy: Daddy, put your bathing suit on. We're going swimming. It's not dark outside.
Me: Who's the boss? You or me.
Kennedy: You.
Me: Thank you for pretending like I'm the boss.

From an early age my greatest influences were women. My dad worked overtime most of my childhood to provide for our family so I spent most of my time with my mom while she was watching other kids. I have three older sisters who all acted like they were my mother, too.

My favorite pastors were women. My first youth pastors were women. My earliest Sunday School teachers were all women.

My connection to God – my faith – was all because of the women influences in my life. We wouldn't even know of Jesus' resurrection if it weren't for the women at the tomb. Women have been – and are – central to my faith development.

When I became a pastor, female empowerment was a topic I often discussed. The importance of female roles in the church was an important subject to me. Women were created to be leaders to be respected; not submissive or seen as "less than" compared to their male counterparts. In marriage counseling, I taught couples that relationships are about mutuality. It is about both partners submitting to one another to meet one another's needs, not one over the other.

I would often express the importance of family time as a preacher too. Prioritizing what we do with our time is an act of worship. It is who and what we are declaring has worth.

When I became a dad, I suddenly wasn't preaching about these topics anymore. *I was living it.*

Instead of preaching about women becoming leaders, I was empowering my wife to become the leader she is now with her career.

Instead of preaching about family time being important, I get to prioritize and balance how our family spends their time (with the help of Shannon).

Becoming a dad of girls, I automatically became more of a feminist, even more so than I was as a preacher. *#GirlDads represent!*

//

It's interesting to me what society norms portray as masculine and feminine.

Making money and being stoic and emotionless and "fulfilling your destiny" are masculine ideals. Taking care of the kids and sharing your feelings are feminine. But this couldn't be farther from the truth for men and women today.

My stay-at-home dad friends have all experienced first-hand other dads calling us "bitches," "sissy babies," or "girly men" for staying home to care for our families and breaking traditional roles. Others will use feminine terms to demean us for doing what we do.

We've all had our masculinity questioned by the outside world — some of us by our families, our parents, the moms at the park, macho dads who don't get it, those who ask if we're babysitting or insult us because we don't make any money or ask us when we're going to get a real job. We are a group of dads who have taken on a non-traditional role and said, *"Forget what the outside world says about masculinity! I'm doing this and I'm going to be damn good at it!"*

Those who would call us dads "girly men" for lifting the women and children in our lives up don't understand that real men are those who do exactly that. Real men treat women with admiration and know a successful woman isn't intimidating.

For myself and dads like me, we get to impress others when they find out we fixed our daughter's hair every day. We take great pride in hearing how kind, respectful, and strong our kids are. Our masculinity is defined by ensuring as fathers that our children are respected by the outside world. Our masculinity is defined by being the most active, involved, nurturing, teaching, caring dads we can be. Making our family life #1 is how we become real men.

In The National At-Home Dad Network, we are able to share our feelings and frustrations and ask for advice in a safe place. For dads to share their feelings on parenting isn't something to be ashamed of. We don't need to "man up." Truth is we are demonstrating our strength as men by having the courage to share the depths of our hearts. We are admitting that our job as parents is hard and we can't do this on our own. We're turning to other men who have been around the block and know a thing or two. It's cowardly to think we *can't* be vulnerable, or weak, or have a bad day, or must keep our feelings bottled up inside.

It takes a real man to take on this job in the first place, breaking traditional barriers. To seek fellowship from other men doing the same thing is strength. We know what it takes to be a man, husband, and father and I believe we are the most masculine men of them all because we've redefined it as pioneers for the whole world to see.

//

One of the comments that really bothers me is when we talk about "motherly instincts" as if dads don't have the capability of knowing when their child is sick or in need of food or a diaper change. When dads are around their children often, we know just as well by our child's body language what they need. It's not a trait only mothers are blessed with.

One of my proudest moments and vindication of my role as a stay-at-home dad was when our friends, Brett and Mary, had issues with their son's daycare and they asked me to watch him for a few weeks until they could transition him to a new daycare. This mattered greatly to me because it showed they trusted me as a father to give the proper care for their son just as well as any mother could. Thank you guys for trusting my fatherly instincts!

//

Shannon and I understand that taking care of the kids is the *parent's* job. Male or female, working parent or not – it is the joint responsibility of both parents to care for their children. Marriage and parenting is a team effort. Spouses should show mutual respect for each other like a wrestling match, where you tag your partner in when you need a break from being in the ring.

Shannon has come home to screaming children and me standing still with a blank stare.

"Long day?"

I don't even have to say anything and she knows I need a break. She'll take the baby from my arms and tell me to make myself a drink and go hide upstairs.

She has come home from a long day at work too and immediately headed to the bathtub. I bring her a big glass of wine because body language says it all.

We're a team and we have a mutual respect for one another.

We have an understanding in our marriage and our job roles. When it comes to cooking, cleaning, finances, caring for the children, caring for one another, taking time alone, and whatever life brings to the table, we work together to make sure we are taken care of as individuals and as a family. We bring balance to each other's chaos.

Some families have acted as if the person who makes the money controls the finances, but Shannon and I definitely don't work that way. We make financial decisions together. It's not her money or my money — *it's our money*. I've never once felt guilty about buying something for myself and neither has Shannon because we have a mutual understanding of what we expect from one another.

I'm not saying we are perfect in any fashion. Like any marriage we have made mistakes that have upset one another, either with raising our child or with finances, but we have learned from those mistakes and made our marriage and lives stronger.

I hear from other dads on occasion that they don't have it in them to do the job I do. I get it. Shannon and I both know that she couldn't be a stay-at-home mom. She's not programmed that way.

Every mom and every dad are different and you have to decide what is best for your family. Not every dad would do well as a stay-at-home parent, *but* I do fully believe that *every* dad should make an effort to take a more active role as a husband and a father!

As the late Supreme Court Justice, Ruth Bader Ginsburg, said:

"Women will have achieved true equality when men share with them the responsibility of bringing up the next generation." [18]

//

When Shannon was pregnant with Reagan and I told others I was about to be the father of two girls, the reaction was "poor daddy" like having a boy is an achievement and having a girl is a failure.

But they don't get it at all.

My masculinity is now defined by being a feminist father. I am empowered by empowering them. The stay-at-home dads of The National At-Home Network and dads likes us have redefined masculinity. We are pioneers for something new. It can be as small as showing young girls movies that represent women as leaders or superheroes or it can be as big as fighting for equal pay for women in the work place.

I love the day and age my daughters are growing up in. As a young boy, I never thought about the lack of representation of females, or people of color, or LGBT persons in film or real life because that didn't apply to me. But now that I am fixing my daughters' hair every morning it has made me pay attention to how girls are represented in the outside world because that is how my daughters could be seen.

Now I realize there is a much bigger world outside of my white, straight, male self.

I love seeing representation being more diverse today.

I love that my girls are growing up with girl Jedis like Rey in *Star Wars*[19] films. (We may or may not have named Reagan so I could call her Rey for short. *Shhh! Don't tell Shannon I said that!*) My girls see women superheroes – and not just women superheroes who are supporting characters but the main title characters of their own films!

They see girls in real life like Meghan Markle who is a person of color who became royalty – and not only that but she and Prince Harry left the royal family to pursue what was best for their own immediate family. What a message of not settling for the norm, but doing what's best for your family!

And now my daughters get to grow up in a country where a woman has become Vice President of The United States of America. What a real life example of dreams becoming reality! Kamala Harris has joined the history books and has instantly become an inspiration for little girls around the world.

When Joe Biden was announced as the president elect, my first thought immediately went to Kamala Harris being the first female vice president. No matter what our political views are, we should celebrate the first Female Vice President in history!

Before Kennedy went to bed the night after their victory speech, I got her attention and made her look me in the eye and I said, "You might not remember tonight, but I will. Today the first Woman Vice President was elected. Daddy's book is about raising presidents – about how you and Reagan can be president someday, like your namesakes, the presidents you were named after. Before today, it was just a dream for a girl to be president and today a GIRL is the VICE PRESIDENT!"

Kennedy's response was, "Wow! Daddy, do I have to brush my teeth? I'm really tired."

//

For parents of boys, you all have the same responsibility – if not more – to teach your boys to respect and empower women and allow space for the women in our lives to make their own decisions about their well-being, careers, and families. It is your responsibility to teach boys that masculinity is caring for the women in their lives and not to feel threatened by the powerful differences a woman has.

Girls are not sissies; girls are superheroes too. Girls are not objects to be controlled; girls are people to be treated with the highest reverence.

And boys are not "girly men" for playing with dolls or wanting a kitchen playset. This could very well be their job when they grow up. And no matter what, they should become men who treat caring for their families as their first responsibility.

My job as a dad is to show my girls how they should be treated by their future partner by being the best husband to my wife. I get to show my girls how they should have a partner who does everything in their power to put them first, someone who works together with them to care for their family. Just like their mama, they shall never be considered as an accessory to a man. They are independent women who demand respect and embody what girl power looks like.

I get to show my daughters how I respect their mom and treat her like the queen she is. I don't just tell my girls they should feel empowered as women, but I get to show them how powerful and hard-working their mommy is. They can dress up like mommy in her work clothes and work shoes and find meaning and respect in being just like mommy. They get to see how powerful and hard-working their mommy is and know they can be just like her.

Mommy is the definition of power and success.

I'm not "poor daddy" for being a girl dad or supporting my wife's career.

My greatest achievement IS being a girl dad and caring for my three girls and helping them to be everything they've been created to be.

As for me and my household, my future is female. And I'm damn proud of that fact.

Chapter 8
My Parenting Complaints are Outweighing My Joy

Shannon and I are really honest when it comes to the struggles of parenthood.

Sometimes too honest.

Shannon said while others have been in her office they'll see pictures of our girls and comment about how beautiful they are.

"Yeah, but they're trouble."
"Yeah, but they're rotten."
"Yeah, but they're a handful."
"Yeah, but they're a hot mess express."

I once told Shannon on the way home from a beach trip with friends that I think we complain too much. When you're with a group of parents, it's natural to vent about your children or spouses, but when you speak too negatively it starts to leak into how you treat them.

I was speaking with one of our friends once about how I just need a break. As a stay-at-home dad, I'm always with my family. When you're at home with a baby, you never catch a break. You're always exhausted and dealing with a screaming baby in one ear and cleaning bottles and cleaning the house and tending to the other kid who doesn't listen to pick up her things and she is always asking a million questions while preparing dinner and the laundry load is never-ending.

Even on this beach trip, it was the same chaos. As someone said to me, "Vacation with kids isn't a vacation; it's a trip." Life with kids is a trip. It's a non-stop ride of moving from one place to the other with little-to-no down time. Even when you have down time you can't stop thinking about all the things that need to get done and you can't turn your brain off.

Parenting is the most difficult job at times.

So, when we are with our friends, I typically use humor to describe dealing with our kids because I know they can relate. I'll tell the story about how my five year old daughter wiped her own ass only to leave poop-soaked toilet paper in her panties that fell onto the floor for her crawling sister to almost put in her mouth before I found it. It's amazing how many stories deal with poop or vomit. Many comedians use stories on parenting because the struggle is real for all of us. And with the real, raw, honest truth of parenting we can see the humor amidst the chaos.

Yet, I wonder how much our kids pick up on our "honesty." When someone comments on how beautiful our daughter is in front of her, and we respond with "Yeah, but she's a hot mess express," what does that do to her self-esteem? We can't take a compliment without overshadowing something positive with something negative. This could have lasting effects if we're not careful. The last thing we would ever want is to make our daughter feel anything but positive about how wonderful she is and special to us and to those around her. If all she heard was our negativity and honesty about the struggles of parenting that would be devastating.

It also affects us. One night the baby was screaming – as she usually was – when Shannon phoned on her way home from work. The five-year-old was pouting because she did not get her way for something. We've been struggling with her attitude and poor listening lately. Shannon asked, "Do I need to let you go to tend to the girls?"

"What's the point? They're going to be upset anyway."

Then Shannon responded, "Maybe we need to be more appreciative of our girls. Maybe our negativity is affecting their attitude – not to mention our own."

We forget that Shannon had three miscarriages before we had Kennedy. We forget how much we longed to be parents.

Sometimes we forget how it felt seeing pictures of babies on social media, and not being able to have that in our own lives. We longed for poopy diapers because that meant we had a child of our own. We longed to hear screaming or for a lack of sleep because that meant we had a baby to hold. In some ways our poor attitude towards parenting is selfish because of all those who wish they were as blessed as us. Our negative, "honest" attitude is selfish because it's robbing us of the joy of being parents. We are blessed to have two beautiful, smart, kind girls.

We should constantly be reminded of how sweet our daughters are.

Kennedy is a great friend and helper to those in need. It's amazing to hear stories from other parents and her teachers of how helpful and sweet she is to her friends when they are upset. She is a great kid, and when we get caught up in the day-to-day chaos we forget that. She puts up with a lot being a big sister, and we sometimes take her for granted. Not sometimes. We *often* take her for granted.

And since we are *not* having any more kids, this baby phase is the last baby phase we will have as parents. Soon we'll long for that poopy diaper blowout because it means we'll still have that little baby snuggle and those cute, squishy cheeks. We should soak up every moment – even the tiresome, disgusting ones – because they'll be gone in the blink of an eye.

Maybe the break we need isn't to take time away from our kids (although all parents need that sometimes).

Maybe what I really need in my day-to-day life is to change my perspective. I need to remind myself that these two little ones are my precious gems. They are to be adored and praised and cherished daily, just as my wife is. My three girls are my world, and I should speak of them highly and with the utmost respect.

Parenting is tough – the most difficult job in the world – but there has never been a better job. There has never been a better investment. There has never been a better use of our time.

To see a child start to crawl or talk. To see a child start to make friends and ride a bike. To see a child grow into the person they are meant to be. To see a child smile, or hear her laugh, or watch her do what she loves. To see a child – your child – be a shining light in this world. That makes everything worth it.

Let not the struggles of parenting outweigh the intoxicating joy of being a parent.

Chapter 9
My New Best Friend

"Those who would try to make you feel less than who you are...that is the greatest evil."
– Fred Rogers

When the new *Beauty and the Beast*[20] movie was released in 2017, there was some concern over LeFou (played by Josh Gad) being the first openly gay man in a Disney film. Some were worried about how kids would react and others were worried about what Disney is teaching our kids.

The same backlash occurred when the Disney children show, *Doc McStuffins*[21], had two interracial lesbian moms on one episode. *Doc McStuffins* is about a young black girl who speaks to her toys and cares for them as their doctor, just as her mom does as an actual doctor, and her dad is a stay-at-home dad.

Should we be worried about how our kids will react to gay persons? Is it too much for children at such a young age? Is it "stripping them of their innocence"?

I was eat lunching at a local fast food restaurant with my daughter who was 4 going on 14 at the time. Just as she does every time we are in a public place, she meets someone who is close to her age and declares: "Daddy, meet my new best friend!"

As much as I try to teach her about "stranger danger," I love her sweet, little heart and how she immediately brings someone new into her world.

As I was trying to take a break from my fireball whirlwind of a 4-year old, her new best friend was taking her over to her booth because she needed to ask her parents a question and get a drink of apple juice. The little girl left her parents to go back to the playground to play, but Kennedy wasn't done talking to them. I mean, she can't just be best friends with the little girl. Everyone is her new best friend!

She said to her parents, "My friend's two mommies…" and continued with her question.

I smiled from across the restaurant. There was no awkwardness or judgment from her saying "two mommies." My daughter didn't even know the word lesbian. And yet she saw her friend had two mommies and didn't think anything of it. It was natural. It was innocent.

The opportunity had never come across for me to share with my daughter anything about gay persons, or what this means, or anything on that subject.

We, as parents, are so concerned about teaching our kids right and wrong. We are so concerned about shielding our children from what could take their innocence away from them, but the only thing that can steal that innocence – often times – is us.

Our children *are* innocent when they see something new and different. They are explorers by nature. They are early scientists and philosophers.

The fact that my daughter saw two mommies and saw nothing abnormal destroys any argument for why we shouldn't have LGBT persons and families in children's shows.

See, their presence in those shows isn't even for straight couples and families, first and foremost.

It's for the children of these gay persons. It's for the two mommies to be represented on screen as part of our world. They exist. They exist just as much as soccer dads yell at the referee. They exist just as much as moms worry about their children. They exist so their children can see parents just like them on their favorite TV show.

In *Doc McStuffins*, the mom is the doctor and the dad stays at home with the kids. I am a stay-at-home dad. When I attended my first Home Dad Convention last year, the majority of the stay-at-home dads had spouses who worked in the medical field, as doctors or otherwise. How cool is it for all of these families to see families like theirs represented on a children's television show?

Not to mention, Doc Mc Stuffins' family is African-American. How cool is it to see not just a woman doctor, but an African-American woman doctor? These families exist and to have themselves represented shows young children that these families can exist – and they do exist.

LeFou in *Beauty and the Beast*, while providing some comic relief, also provided some hope to that young boy who saw LeFou's gayness and learned it was okay to be different. Scratch that. Let me say it another way: If we have better representation of people like LeFou, a young boy will just see it's okay to be himself. Being gay will no longer be different. Being gay will be a natural way of being.

Something seems abnormal or different because we don't know it exists. Representation changes that. It helps remove prejudices when you see women and persons of color as doctors and you know they are kind and powerful and worthy of our attention. It helps remove stereotypes when you see a gay character is as funny and lovable as anyone else. It helps change cultures when we see a new world come to life as it did in the film *Black Panther*.

Black Panther[22] (2018) was a cultural revolution. This superhero film was more than a superhero film. This film had a primarily African American cast. In Wakanda, the fictional country in Africa where the film takes place, these Black men and women have the most powerful country in the world. Wakanda has the leading technology and scientists, which has been hidden from the rest of the world.

Its leading scientist is a young Black girl, Shuri, who is the sister of the king. Shuri was my favorite character in the film. She was funny and strong and smart and witty. What a powerful message it would send to a young Black girl to see a character like herself be the smartest person in the most powerful country in the world with the best technology in the world! The power to believe in yourself sometimes comes from these metaphorical stories which show us this can be possible. It's more than make-believe. It's a metaphor for how we can be superheroes too. These stories teach us lessons of how we can treat people and make a difference.

When Chadwick Boseman, the actor who played T'Challa/Black Panther, died this year I was heartbroken. Boseman played many famous Black persons, such as James Brown, Jackie Robinson, and Thurgood Marshall. He made these characters real for the big screen with such raw authenticity. I grieved his death because Boseman was a symbol of hope. During times of racial tension and concerns with police brutality this year, I have been looking forward to Black Panther 2 coming out soon because we *need* a little metaphorical hope from what has become one of the greatest superhero films in recent years.

I know the filmmakers will do justice to the death of the actor who played their title character, but it pains me greatly that Boseman cannot continue his work that was such an inspiration. He was a symbol of hope because Black children wanted to be him, the story he embodied was a revolution, and this story for the first time showed Black superheroes as the most powerful persons in the world.

There was a viral video of Black men getting excited about the *Black Panther* film's poster and it's primarily Black cast being shown on the poster. They said, "Do you see this?! This is how white people feel all the time!" White people – whether we realize it or not – are used to being portrayed as superheroes or doctors or people of incredible power from an incredible culture. *Black Panther* is more than a film – it's a cultural revolution – because it created a culture where Black persons are the most powerful. This kind of representation shows us that the dream, the metaphorical world on this big screen, can be a reality. Black persons can believe in a world where they are not just the supporting cast; they are the lead actor. They are the president, the leader of this world, the richest, the smartest, the most powerful, the best.

Telling stories where both someone can see themselves in the story and can be inspired to be a better person is the central focus of what telling stories is all about.

This is important to us as parents because when our children see stories that include them this helps to motivate them to be like the character they see in these stories. And if they see characters who are different than them, this opens up doors to teach them that there is a beautiful, diverse world outside of ourselves that deserves our kindness and respect. We have a responsibility to build up and protect all of God's children.

As a United Methodist pastor I was distraught when the United Methodist Church decided not to change its language on homosexuality in 2018. The UMC Book of Discipline states that "Homosexuality is incompatible with Christian teaching." Even though the United States government accepts gay marriage, the United Methodist Church (UMC) decided against it. Also, it denied the possibility of gay persons being ordained ministers in the UMC.

These decisions were heartbreaking for me and many of my friends at that time. I hoped that a denomination as big as the UMC would make a progressive stance forward. Since the decision, there has been a rebellion in many individual UMC churches in the United States. They have declared that their churches will be accepting and inclusive no matter what the wider UMC decided. They will continue to fight for the language to be changed and for acceptance of all persons to be allowed the same rights. Some UMC pastors have spoken out against this decision by the world-wide church. Some have even gone as far as relinquishing their ordination credentials because they can no longer be a part of a church that isn't inclusive for all.

Telling stories is one thing because it helps to make dreams a reality. But seeing these dreams become reality is a whole other realm. I would love to see a church be truly inclusive of all because that is how I think Jesus lived his life. He loved the outcasts and the ones the world loves to hate. He took the time to reach out to people of different cultures and genders and religions than his own. He brought to light persons who were otherwise ignored. He was a cultural revolution in real life. He showed us how we could show grace and love those we would have otherwise ignored.

The reality that I have friends who are not accepted for who they are is disheartening. The reality that there are teenagers, or even young children, who are depressed or suicidal because of who they are is horrific. The fact that kids are being bullied because of who some people believe they are is atrocious.

While I was upset about the state of things in the church back in 2018, I went to a birthday party for one of my daughter's friends. My daughter had kids in her class who were bilingual, who were from other cultures, who were of a different race or religion, and/or who had gay parents. The greatest compliment I could ever receive about my daughter is each of her friend's parents tell my wife and I how kind she is. All these kids from various backgrounds and diverse families are her "new best friend."

I realized something as I looked at all her friends and their parents at this birthday party. The world I had dreamed of where everyone is accepted for who they are and loved no matter what their family looks like was represented at this party. We don't treat the gay parents as "the gay parents;" they are parents trying to raise their kids just like the rest of us. They gave great advice and they were fun to be around and we still call them friends, just like our daughter calls their kids her friends. In our circle, they are already accepted and loved as one of us. They are represented because they are a part of our reality.

What the Church had decided is to continue a historical misconception about a reality that simply doesn't exist anymore. The conversation is over. We are not talking about whether gay persons should be married; they already are, and their marriages together are beautiful. We are not talking about whether gay persons should be fathers or mothers together; they already are, and they are doing a damn good job at it (many better than any heterosexual parents). We don't need to have that conversation of inclusion and representation at our birthday party because we already live in the new world we hoped we would create for our children.

Those two mommies my daughter saw at Chick-fil-a already exist. My daughter knows it. She knew it before I could tell her. Their representation on the big or little screen only shows the rest of us that they exist too. It shows that they can exist, and they will exist, and they do exist.

The two daddies at the birthday party are simply a welcome part of our lives, as well as the diverse group of families in my daughter's class.

I love the friends we have at this birthday party. They are one of us. And we will go to bat for any one of them or their children if someone is unkind to them or makes them feel less than who they are. Because that is what we do for our friends.

Just as my daughter immediately makes a new best friend with everyone she meets, may we do the same.

And may we be sure to teach our children how important it is to define success the way Mr. Rogers does.

As Fred Rogers says, "There are three rules to success. The first is to be kind. The second is to be kind. The third is to be kind." [23]

Chapter 10
Beloved

Most of our family is in the Fort Worth area in Texas. My parents, my three older sisters and each of their families, Shannon's mom, Shannon's dad & wife and their family, Shannon's sister and her family, and Shannon's maternal grandma all live in Texas.

It's so much easier when a few of them come visit us in Florida because when we go to Texas we're strapped for time trying to make time for everyone. Arranging schedules to see everyone is really stressful. Our friends in Texas know now that it is impossible to make time for them on our visits because our family will disown us if they don't get sufficient time with their grandbabies/nieces/cousins.

In 2016, I made a two week trip on my own with two-year old (almost three) Kennedy to visit everyone in Texas. I left feeling both blessed for the time we had with them and empty because I wish we had more time with each family member and friend, just as it is on every trip.

This trip was especially significant because I was able to watch the family dynamics through the eyes of a two-year old. As her dad, I was able to get her to stop crying as we leave one family member because I was able to tell her who we were going to visit next. But what was interesting was to hear Kennedy talk about each person she's just visited to the other person she was visiting now or who she's going to visit next. For her, each family member and friend are all one, big family. We're not the Clarks and Lemons and Phipps and Ebels and Daileys and Prices and Mills and Piercys and Queretaros families. We're all family.

It was simply beautiful to see the love she has for everyone. And the love everyone has for her.

Our friends were her uncles & aunts as far as she was concerned. Her excitement to see everyone & the laughter & cuddles she shares with each person would take your breath away.

One lesson I wanted to teach her is to include everyone like they are family. *This two-year-old embodied that before I could teach it to her!*

She taught *me* how to include everyone as family.

My daughter doesn't know the different family dynamics. She didn't know some people were divorced when she talked about one to the other. She didn't know some people weren't on a talking basis when she talked about one to the other. There was nothing but excitement and love for each person.

Every person was beloved. This toddler taught me a little more about God and God's vision for family. In a world divided by who we are and who we are not, this cute, curly-haired girl lived in a world where we are all family.

Jesus says we should enter the kingdom of heaven with the heart of a child. My child taught me why he said that.

When you take all the bitterness and the hatred and the fear away, we're brothers and sisters and daughters and sons and fathers and mothers and uncles and aunts and cousins and friends and wives and husbands and partners. We're family.

//

Towards the end of that same trip, I held my daughter close to my chest as I watched the news coverage with Shannon's dad, Kip, and bonus mom, Lynn. (Kennedy was watching Sofia the First not the news.) It was June 12, 2016.

A 29-year old man shot and killed 49 people and wounded 53 others in a mass shooting at Pulse Night Club, a gay night club. I couldn't help but think about all the family members and friends who wouldn't hold their loved ones again.

Pulse Night Club is just down the street from the hospital where Reagan was born two years later in 2018 in Orlando.

That morning I thought about the gay persons who hadn't told their family members who they really were out of fear and now their family might find out they're gay as they also hear they've been a victim of this senseless violence.

I thought about my friends who would be ministering to their congregations that morning, hopefully bringing healing at a time when our country is very confused and in pain (not much different than today).

I thought about my friends who were youth ministers, many who were on mission trips all over the country that week, and the questions the teenagers might have that week after the horrific events in Orlando.

When I was a teenager, I thought being gay was weird. I didn't understand it. When I was told it was a sin, it was easy for me to accept because that wasn't me. It was different.

As I got older and I saw such hatred that was being poured out to a group of people, my thinking changed.

The God I know is a God of love who would do anything to show His children how much he loves them.

And so I've recognized that I need to stand up against such hatred that causes a group of people to be hated. And bullied. And *murdered*. They might be different but They. Are. Family.

And I will look at them as I look at my own daughter. With love. As family.

//

I once gave the Eulogy at the funeral of a 26-year old who was on his motorcycle and was hit by a 16-year old in a car and died. The young man and his family were members at the church I was a pastor of in Reddick, Florida. I had never officiated a funeral for someone so young. After I gave the Eulogy, a few other friends said a few words, then his brother, and finally his dad.

His dad is a stoic Marine who doesn't get emotional. He is an all-around great guy. His dad said how much he loved and was proud of his son and how he loved spending time with him as an adult and seeing his son's wisdom. He then said his favorite moment in 26 years was with his son as a baby singing, "You are my Sunshine." He then had the courage to sing the entire song and as soon as he finished, he began weeping uncontrollably. I mean, hardcore weeping where others came up to be with him and hold him.

There wasn't a dry eye in the place. *I will never forget that uncontrollable sorrow.*

My wife and I sing that song every day to Kennedy on the way to school. We sing that song to Reagan every night before she falls asleep.

In those moments we want to pull our hair out as parents, I'll remember this father's grief, and soak up every moment, and give my kid an extra hug.

I'll remember the families who have lost loved ones because of senseless violence due to hatred and racism and bigotry throughout the years. And vow to teach my kids to be kind always.

I hope that tomorrow we don't forget the tragedies that happened yesterday that remind us to hold our children close.

I hope we can look at each other the way my daughter sees all of you.

As beloved members of her family.

Chapter 11
Friendship Day

Kennedy took a gymnastics class for a few months when she was four years old. Each week they had a different theme. One particular day the theme was "Friendship." She had already made a friend before class – a curly-haired girl much like herself. They talked about the rain outside and exchanged names. They played with a train together and told the boy next to them, "You're a boy!" when he tried to join them.

So, when the gymnastics teacher asked her to pick a friend she already knew who she would pick. Well, it soon became obvious to me that her friend was the "rebel" who wanted to always do the opposite of what the teacher said. "Oh great," I muttered under my breath.

Throughout the beginning of class, Kennedy tried to do the activity she was asked to do by the teacher while her friend was aloof doing whatever she chose to. Luckily, for the gymnastics portion she was in a different group than her friend so she was more focused.

At the end of the class, the children were asked to pair back up with their friends. Kennedy continually tried to do what the teacher asked, but when her friend wanted to sit on the side of the gym she joined her. I wanted to step in and tell her to do what she's been told but instead I watched to see this play out.

When the teacher asked them to rejoin the group, Kennedy tried pulling her friend's arm and convincing her to do what they're told. But her friend wouldn't budge. Conflicted on whether to obey the teacher or stay with her friend, she chose to stay with her friend. She also started to pout because she knew she wasn't doing what she was supposed to.

After class, I did the parent thing by telling her she needs to listen to her teachers and be a leader even when her friends choose not to. But my heart smiled because on a day focused on friendship she chose to sit with her friend even when she knew there would be consequences. She knew obeying the teacher was the right thing to do and the activity the rest of the class was doing was more fun, but she wouldn't leave her friend alone. I secretly hope she will always be as devoted and compassionate to her friends (and maybe she'll get better at convincing them to rejoin the group too).

May we all be a rebellious friend such as this.

Chapter 12
Chrysalis

> *"Nature does not proceed by leaps and bounds." – Carolus Linnaeus, 1751[24]*

I felt like the terrible parent.

Kennedy had been having a terrible week. She was lying to us about washing her hands or denying when she was doing something wrong. She was making poor, dangerous choices, like crawling in her baby sister's crib or stacking multiple step stools on top of her hope chest so she could pull the chain hanging from her fan – and nearly falling on her sister in the process. As I returned home from running an errand and Shannon left for a girl's night, I was suddenly stuck with a difficult decision.

In 2018, we had moved to Orlando and our new home was five miles from Disneyworld.

Kennedy could see the fireworks at Magic Kingdom from her bedroom window. Disney became our second home as we went there as often as we could.

I had planned an evening of fun going to Disney with Kennedy and Reagan while mommy was hanging out with her friends. I called my buddy Richard for moral support to be the strong disciplinarian and he said I should skip our evening of fun to Disney to teach her a lesson. We did. I told Kennedy to get in the car to go with me to get fast food for dinner because I didn't have anything planned. She tried to make her case for Disney still. I told her she needed to zip it.

"I don't want to hear another word!"

I was upset we couldn't have fun, too. The baby was screaming, and Kennedy and I just glared at each other through the rear view mirror because we both had ruined each other's day.

Both kids fell asleep and it was peace and quiet in the car. I thought about driving for hours just to keep both kids asleep. I picked up tacos. Kennedy woke up and wanted her taco immediately.

I came to the point in the road where one way was home and the other was Disney. I tried to stay strong but at the last second I turned towards Disney.

Kennedy knew immediately where we were going.

"Daddy, where are you going?! I thought we were going home."

We talked again about making good choices on the way to the park. We went to see a nighttime show, *Fantasmic*, we hadn't seen before at Disney's Hollywood Studios. And it was an awesome time with the girls.

I felt like the pushover dad or the participation trophy parent with no discipline or consequences. But grace was central to my parents when they were raising me and I always vowed it would be central to me as a parent.

Kennedy knew what she had lost when she got so upset, she fell asleep in the car. She had already accepted her fate, that we were going home to pout with our crappy tacos. But then we made a different turn to a different destination.

There will be time for more consequences. But grace that night was receiving what we don't deserve. Kennedy finally learned that lesson, that she didn't deserve to have fun, but fun still arrived when she least expected it. Grace is when we thought a bland life was planned for us because that's what we deserved, but something magical is our destination.

//

Every parent who has ever brought a newborn home from the hospital has the same thought:

They trust me to take this precious kid home and care for it? Doesn't this thing come with an instruction manual?

The most important job we will ever have comes with no instruction manual because every child is different. Every child starts talking and walking differently. Every child learns differently. Every child has different personalities. Every child grows differently. Every child requires discipline differently.

This doesn't stop experienced parents from giving us advice. Sometimes we want their advice and sometimes we want to figure out things on our own. To the grandparents who have children who are grown and raised – take a step back. Sometimes new parents like – and need – the journey of figuring things out on their own.

Every parent is different. Every parenting style is different. Parents make hard decisions every day on the best way to care for their child. Most of it is trial and error to figure out what works best for your child and your family. Unique parents making unique decisions for their unique child.

Parents make just as many mistakes as their children do. We cry when we just screamed at our child for misbehaving. We feel guilty for not living up to the same standards as the parent next door. We worry about everything from what food to give our child, how much screen time to allow, what types of activities to have our child do, how to help them get the most out of their schooling, and how to make sure they don't grow up to be jerks.

//

What no one can prepare us for is getting the kids ready for school. Getting the child to wake up, take a bath, get dressed, brush their teeth, fix their hair, eat breakfast, prepare their lunch, feed the baby, dress the baby, remember the baby's diaper bag, remember the child's lunch, remember the child's homework, remember their fancy school project, remember that you forgot it's freaking Spirit Week and your child has to change clothes, remember that you need to get dressed too, tell your child to put on her shoes fifty times because it's time to go, remembering to get her water bottle, then telling her to turn the television off and putting her shoes at her feet so she'll actually put them on, and finally getting in the car and strapping the baby in her car seat and telling the kid to put her seat belt on because the car is moving and taking a breath as you sit in the car line at school for fifteen minutes.

"I love you Kennedy. Listen to your teachers, be nice to your friends, and be awesome every day."

Your child makes it inside the school doors two minutes before the final bell rings.

The morning routine is one of the hardest parts of being a parent. It's a full-time job in itself. You might get some down time in the afternoon when the baby is napping but that is your reward for the lethal combination of getting the kids out the door in the morning and the witching hour after school.

Today, I prepare lunch for the next day directly after we get home from school and bathe the children the night before, so the morning routine is slightly less stressful. Luckily Kennedy is independent enough now that she knows what is expected of her in the morning. *But for some reason she still can't remember to put her shoes on.*

Every day we grow as parents just as our kids grow. It's a process of deciding what type of parent we will be and molding our kids to be who we hope they will be every morning and every night.

//

Caterpillars go through a process called chrysalis. The chrysalis is the shell the caterpillar is wrapped in as it is molded into a butterfly. The caterpillar releases digestive juices to break down itself into molecules. The remaining cells reorganize itself into an adult butterfly.

Then, after a period of metamorphosis, the butterfly excretes the rest of its juices to complete metamorphosis. It then emerges out of its shell with wings spread. It pumps fluid through its wing veins to fully expand.

//

You wouldn't know it now, but Kennedy had a speech delay that we first noticed when she was one year old. Shannon noticed it immediately but I was in denial. My heart sunk the first time we were putting her into speech therapy and a consultant said she has "special needs."

Special needs children shouldn't have a negative stigmatism for any parent. Every child is different, and every child grows differently. Every child is talented in some way too, and it is about finding your child's gifts. It's meeting their needs so they can grow and learn to fly.

Kennedy had awesome teachers at an early age who helped with her speech development. Teachers like Ms. Andrea and Ms. Williams and her speech therapist, Ms. Kelli.

In addition to her speech therapy, I think what really helped her to come out of her shell was our first trip to Disneyworld in 2016 (we lived in Kentucky at the time). Kennedy had been scared of people in costume like Santa Claus or the Easter Bunny, but when she saw Mickey Mouse and the princesses, it was just as magical as you might imagine. She adored talking to them and telling them her life story.

It was like a little Disney magic – or pixie dust – helped her start talking.

Once this kid started talking, she never stopped. Anyone who said, "Oh my, you are so cute…" better be prepared to have this little girl talk their ear off! One time when we were on an airplane everyone knew her by name because she was telling everyone stories. She blossomed into such a social butterfly.

On one of our first trips to Disney after our move to Orlando, Kennedy befriended a group of girls from Brazil. I have a picture of all these teenage girls with their green Disney trip shirts circled around Kennedy hanging on her every word. These girls didn't even speak much English but they were listening to my daughter tell them stories and it was captivating.

No matter what language someone spoke or what country they were from or what race someone was, this cute little girl befriended everyone. She has been a joy to watch.

What she lacked in communicating when she was young, she made up for with kindness and befriending everyone she meets.

//

One day in 2019, Shannon braved Disney by herself with both girls. She recalled how she was incredibly nervous and overwhelmed on her own, but they had an amazing day together. And she shared a moment she will never forget with our incredible daughter, Kennedy.

They had boarded the monorail at the Ticket and Transportation Center (TTC) on their way to Magic Kingdom – which can take forever for any parent who has experienced it. It's actually one of the reasons we avoid going to Magic Kingdom because it can take over thirty minutes to get in the park.

This day was different, though. A boy about 8-9 years old was screaming at the top of his lungs and was convinced that his parents tricked him onto a roller coaster and that the monorail was not the correct way to Disney. Shannon watched several people walk into the monorail cabin and then promptly exit after hearing the boy's screams but she openly walked in and tried to help the parents as much as she could.

The boy's mother shared that he was autistic. She asked Shannon if they could walk to Disney from the TTC in a desperate attempt to escape this madness and Shannon sadly shared that wasn't possible. The parents had his sisters block the doorway and somehow by the grace of God were able to keep him from jumping out before the door closed.

Shannon was cautious about how Kennedy would respond but instead of being scared or just staring like most kids, she walked up to him as the monorail took off and showed him her Cinderella Castle lanyard full of pins as a way to distract him. Shannon was scared he might kick or hit her with the violent state he was in, but the boy immediately calmed down and enjoyed talking to her. His parents were also visibly relieved after holding him back.

After what must have seemed like hours into the ride for this family, Kennedy offered the boy to pick out his favorite pin off of her lanyard and to keep it as his first pin for trading with cast members throughout the day. The boy picked an Elsa pin and put it on his own lanyard. He was overjoyed.

The mother of the boy and Shannon both were in tears and it's a moment for our family to cherish forever. Kennedy and Shannon talked a lot about how she made someone's day very special.

Shannon was beaming with pride at the lesson of kindness and generosity she witnessed from our own daughter that day.

//

We first witnessed this kindness from Kennedy after we returned from that first trip to Disney back in 2016 and her speech started to progress. There was a young girl like her who had a speech delay in her class. She was having trouble communicating to the teachers what she needed and she was getting visibly upset. But Kennedy understood her. She was able to interpret for the teachers what this girl was saying because they shared a speech delay.

Kennedy has had this gift of caring for children in need. Her teachers throughout the years have always spoke highly of her for caring for children when they are crying and helping them to rejoin the class. Her teachers said they believe she will be a teacher herself when she grows up.

I don't know what my girls will be when they grow up.

At one year old, I think Reagan wants to be in *Frozen 3* and to drink out of sippy cups forever.

At seven years old, Kennedy now wants to be a dancing actress astronaut teacher on a unicorn.

One thing I know for sure is she is a storyteller like her daddy.

//

When Kennedy was in kindergarten in 2019, she told us she needed to wear her special field trip shirt to school the next day. Shannon and I both said there wasn't a field trip that we were aware of but she insisted she needed to wear her shirt to school and we were exhausted so we granted her wishes. She has been right about things in the past that we didn't know about for school because Shannon and I were still in a fog from adjusting to caring for two kids – our strong-willed six year old and even stronger-willed newborn.

Immediately after getting home from school the next day Kennedy began telling me she went on a field trip to the zoo. In a state of shock, I began asking a million questions and called Shannon to share Kennedy's field trip to the zoo. She gave us all the details of the trip, including who was there, the animals they saw, the bus they rode on, and even the funny stories the bus driver told her. She was *very* convincing. She had us fooled so well that we were a little freaked out the school would take them off property without telling us or that we missed the notification (which given our daily chaos at the time was *completely* plausible).

Shannon and I began calling and texting as many kindergarten parents as we could to figure out what had happened and why were unaware of this field trip. We were close to calling the principal and teacher and inquiring how they could take our child off property without our permission.

It wasn't until I told Kennedy that I was going to call her teacher that she freaked out and admitted she lied to us.

I scolded her for lying to us, as Shannon did as well when she made it home from work.

But then I whispered in Shannon's ear:

Our child is a REALLY good storyteller.

Maybe Kennedy will become an author like her daddy.

Parenting is being upset with your child for their actions but then also beaming with pride at the same time because you see part of yourself in them.

//

I know Kennedy and Reagan will have times of growth and adjustment as they get older. Shannon and I also will have times of learning how to balance discipline and grace as we continue our journey as parents. Shannon has always said when the girls become teenagers, I'm in charge of them.

We've all felt like we've lived through 50 years of growth and adjustment during the Coronavirus Pandemic of 2020 and all the stress that's occurred.

For all of us who have lived through 2020, we have definitely learned to appreciate each moment and blessing we have. From schools and teachers, to trips and extracurricular activities, to our time with family and friends, to hugs from loved ones and snuggles from our kids – we've definitely learned this year to not take for granted everything that makes us smile on our journey (even through our masks).

If there's one thing I've learned, it is to appreciate the journey. The moments are so fleeting

With Reagan, I hold her tight and admire her baby features because I know those baby cheeks won't last forever. With

Kennedy, Shannon often reminds me it won't be much longer before she no longer asks us to tuck her into bed.

I look at Kennedy, who now has her two front teeth missing, and Reagan, who is growing new baby teeth, and I know to soak up each moment with my girls.

Before I blink both of these girls will be getting their first car and will be going to college, and getting their heart broken, and finding their true love, and picking their career, and having kids of their own, so now I try to hold these girls tight in their shells as they continue their metamorphosis at this stage in their lives.

Just as Shannon and I continue our own metamorphosis as their parents.

One thing about butterflies: when they first emerge from their chrysalis and spread their beautiful wings, they must wait for their wings to dry before they can fly.

Time sometimes speeds by so fast we don't know how we got here. And at other times when we're ready to fly, we have to wait.

We're reminded to slow down time and wait for our wings to dry.

Nature does not proceed by leaps and bounds.

I don't know what my girls will become when they're older. But just like we pray for them every night, *I know they can be whoever they want to be – and we will love them no matter who they become.*

Growing up is a chrysalis journey that's different for every child. Enjoy the time kids are in their shells because they'll be flying before we know it.

And when it's time for my girls to fly, I'll remind them to put their shoes on.

NOTES

Chapter 1:
1. *Daniel Tiger's Neighborhood.* PBS, 2012. Television.
** I couldn't find a way to fit this in the book, but I decided to include this here for you detailed people to hear one of my favorite stories: I was picking Shannon and her sister, Kacie, up from a concert late at night one evening when Kennedy was 3 years old. We were parked in a parking lot waiting for them to make their way to us when a young college-age woman who must have had too much to drink decided to stop and urinate in between our car and another car. Without missing a beat, Kennedy starts singing Daniel Tiger's song, "If you have to go potty, stop and go right away!" Kennedy and I both started laughing hysterically. I'm glad that young woman didn't pee her pants in the middle of the parking lot.
2. "Can't Stop The Feeling." Album: *Trolls*. Artist: Justin Timberlake. RCA Records, 2016. Song.
3. *The Flintstones.* ABC, 1960. Television.
4. *Jackass.* MTV, 2000. Television.
5. *Star Wars.* 20th Century Fox, 1977. Film.

6. Beast, Lambie, Genie, Mike Wazowski. Beast – character from *Beauty & The Beast.* Disney, 1991. Film. Lambie – character from *Doc McStuffins.* Disney Junior, 2012. Television. Genie – character from *Aladdin.* Disney, 1992. Film. Mike Wazowski – character from *Monsters Inc.* Disney, 2001. Film.

Chapter 2:

7. Clark, Russell. *Loser.* Self-published, 2017.
8. *Paw Patrol*. Nick Junior, 2013. Television.
9. *Doc McStuffins*. Disney Junior, 2012. Television.
10. *Mickey Mouse Clubhouse*. Disney Junior, 2005. Television.

Chapter 3:

11. *Star Wars.* 20th Century Fox, 1977. Film.

Chapter 4:

12. *Catastrophe.* Amazon, 2015. Television.
13. *Paw Patrol*. Nick Junior, 2013. Television.
14. National At-Home Dad Network. Athomedad.org
15. *Bad Moms*. Paramount Pictures, 2016. Film.
16. *Bad Moms 2: A Bad Moms Christmas*. STX Films, 2017. Film.

Chapter 5

Chapter 6:

17. *Man of Steel.* Warner Bros, 2013. Film.

Chapter 7:
18. Ginsburg, Ruth Bader. *The Record. "Constitutionalizing Women's Equality: The Ruth Bader Ginsburg Distinguished Lecture on Women and The Law."* The Association of the Bar of the City of New York, 2001.
19. *Star Wars.* 20th Century Fox, 1977. Film.

Chapter 8

Chapter 9:
20. *Beauty & The Beast.* Disney, 2017. Film.
21. *Doc McStuffins.* Disney Junior, 2012. Television.
22. *Black Panther.* Marvel Studios, 2018. Film.
23. Although this quote is famously credited to Fred Rogers, the writer Henry James is credited with originally saying this.

Chapter 10

Chapter 11

Chapter 12
24. Linnaeus, Carolus. *Philosophia Botanica, edition 1.* Stockholm & Amsterdam, 1751.

Acknowledgments

John Lee, for creating the cover design.

Jim Reeves & Lisa McCulloch, for your diligent help with editing my book.

Dr. Gladys Childs, John Francis, Jonathan Heisey-Grove, and Brock Lusch, thank you so much for writing endorsements for the book.

Our family and friends in Kentucky, Texas, and Florida, we love you all and thank you for your love, support, and friendship.

Shannon, Kennedy, & Reagan, for being the center of my world and my inspiration to continue telling stories.

About the Author

Russell Clark resides in Orlando, Florida with his wife, Shannon, and daughters, Kennedy and Reagan. He graduated with a Masters of Divinity from Brite Divinity School in Fort Worth, Texas and a Bachelor's Degree in Christian Education from Texas Wesleyan University in Fort Worth, Texas. His first book, Loser, is also available on Amazon.com.

Customer Review and Social Media

Please take the time to rate *Raising Presidents* and share your thoughts on Amazon. My hope is this book will be inspirational to tackle the challenges of parenting and a brief escape from the world for you all. If you feel the same way, please share your thoughts on social media and share this book with 1000 of your closest friends.

Connect

Facebook: fb.me/russellclarkauthor
E-mail: russellclarkauthor@yahoo.com

Booking Information

To book Russell for speaking engagements, radio broadcasts, or podcasts, please contact russellclarkauthor@yahoo.com.

Made in the USA
Coppell, TX
19 November 2020